Dear Soldier . . .

Dear Soldier. . .

Letters of encouragement
to service members
around the world

Compiled by
Tawny Archibald Campbell

spring creek
BOOK COMPANY
Provo, Utah

ISBN 978-1-932898-77-4
c. 1

Published by:
Spring Creek Book Company
P.O. Box 50355
Provo, Utah 84605-0355

www.springcreekbooks.com

Cover design by Nicole Cunningham

Printed in the United States of America
10 9 8 7 6 5 4 3 2 1
Printed on acid-free paper

Library of Congress Control Number: 2007929681

DEDICATION

This book is dedicated to the thousands of troops who raised their right arm to the square and promised to God and Country to protect and defend each and every one of us.

It is also dedicated to the mothers, fathers, sons, daughters, husbands and wives of those brave men and women serving in our Armed Forces.

Acknowledgments

This book as been a labor of love, something I have dreamed of doing ever since my husband joined the Army. Now that it is a reality, I would like to thank my husband Joe and my daughter Ceilidha, my parents Ray and Cheri Archibald, my brother Ian and the Harnden family for all the support. Without them we wouldn't have the letters that fill the pages of this book.

I would also like to thank everyone who took the time to write a letter to a service member. I have watched tears roll down the cheeks of these brave men and women as they read your words of kindness and support and have seen smiles spread across bandaged faces as they feel of your love.

This book is written not by a professional author or a team of experts. It is written by people like you and me—people who felt a desire to express their appreciation for the men and women in uniform who put their lives on the line every day. Their service allows us to live where we live, work where we work, worship how we choose, and wake up every morning in the land of the free. These deployed service members miss out on birthdays, holidays, graduations, anniversaries and other special occasions. Many miss out on the birth of a child, and "firsts" like the first steps, first words, first day of school, first date, first dance and so much more.

To these men and women, we salute you, we honor you, we love you, and most of all we support you.

My husband, Joe, is one of these men of uniform, one who has sacrificed so much for the better good. He, like so many others, doesn't do it for the glory or praise; he does it because it is the right thing to do. He stands up and fights so someone else's son or daughter doesn't have to.

Introduction

My husband and I were driving home one October afternoon when out of the blue I turned to Joe and stated, "We are going to spend Christmas this year at the airport." He turned and gave me a "You're serious about this?" look, which quickly turned into a "How creative" nod followed by a resolute sigh and accompanying smile.

"Sounds okay to me," he finally said.

Once I knew he was onboard I started to think about what we were going to do at the airport. You see, I really hadn't thought this through very thoroughly before I blurted out my idea. This was our first Christmas in Germany, and our first Christmas an ocean away from any family, so what better way to spend it than serving others in the same situation?

We contacted the local USO and formed a plan. We would hand out decorated brown paper lunch bags each filled with a Christmas ornament, American candy, German candy, baked treat, poem and a letter written to "Dear Service Member." We thought a hundred or so should suffice. After contacting the local military airport, I realized we would need more like a thousand bags. I thought our idea was going to die as quickly as it was born.

Not knowing where to turn for help, I called up my mom, half a world away in Idaho, and we came up with a plan. My little brother, Ian Archibald, was struggling to finish his Eagle Scout project, so we roped him into helping and dumped a lot of the responsibility stateside on him.

Together we came up with the name "Project Rudolph" and went to work. With the help of another Boy Scout here in Germany, we started talking to schools, retirement homes, youth groups, church groups, families and other people throughout the world. Over the next six weeks we collected enough items to put together over 1,000 Project Rudolph Bags to be handed out to injured service members, those headed to the Middle East and those deployed to Germany.

One of the requirements before handing out the bags was reading all the letters, both from youth and adults, to make sure they were appropriate for our military members. As I read through the close to 2,000 letters, some brought tears to my eyes and others made me laugh. No matter what they said, each letter sent a message; our troops were loved, supported and missed. I felt selfish reading all these letters, knowing there were hundreds and thousands of people who could benefit from these words of encouragement, so I started to copy them down hoping that somehow I could find a way to share these letters with others.

Soon I had enough for a book—this book. It is intended to bring smiles, cheer, and warm fuzzies to service members, and also to the families, friends and loved ones who support them.

But the story doesn't end here. Project Rudolph is now an annual event and year-round we are collecting letters to hand out over the holidays. We have also started Operation Angel where we hand out "Angel Baggies" to service members at Landstuhl Regional Medical Center in Germany, the hospital that treats all service members medically evacuated out of the Iraq, Kuwait and Afghanistan. We would love to include letters of support in each of the Angel Baggies as well.

If you would like to assist by contributing a letter for a Project Rudolph Bag or an Angel Baggie, you may contact Tawny Campbell at taznjo@hotmail.com, visit www.projectrudolph.homestead.com or www.operationangel.homestead.com.

Or mail your letters to:
Military Letters of Support
c/o the Archibalds
600 South Wilson
Oakley, Idaho 83346

Dear Soldier . . .

Dear Soldiers,

It must be hard serving in the military. I should know—my dad was in the Navy and he lived through thick and thin. It must hurt not being able to see your family. It hurts getting injured. I know—I got ran over by a lawnmower. It hurts.

Sincerely yours,
Stormie W.

Dear Service Person,

I think you are a great person. Thanks for fighting in the war and helping us be free. I hope you like what I sent you. I think it might be hard going over there and fighting for our families and other people. Someday I might go to war. I am still thinking about it. I am glad that you fought for our country. Thanks a lot! I hope you have a Merry Christmas! I'm sure I will have a great one, and you should, too! I really appreciate all that you did for us! Thanks!

Alexis
4th grader from (Malta) Idaho

Merry Christmas!

Thank you for everything that you have done to keep this country safe. I don't think that I could leave my family and go to a foreign country and fight for my country. I appreciate everything that you and many others have done!

Sincerely,
Robert M.
Nampa, Idaho

Dear U.S. Serviceman,

Thank you for protecting our country and making the sacrifice. You are in our prayers and our hearts and the Lord is watching you. We are thankful for the things you do. Your family must miss you. Keep your mind strong and follow your heart. If you have them read the [scriptures], it's a powerful thing; a chapter a day keeps the devil away. That's what my quorum says, anyway. Be safe.

Sincerely,
Jacob McBride
Oakley, Idaho

Dear servicemen,

Thank you for sacrificing everything you have for us. We are so thankful for everything you do. A serviceman named Aaron Hart came and spoke to my [church] about what is going on over in Iraq. He told us about their latest election and how people wanted freedom so bad that to keep people from voting twice, they had to dip their thumbs in purple ink. Anyway, thank you for all that you have done. We appreciate all that you guys do.

Oakley, Idaho

You are my friend for helping our country.

Raft River Elementary School

Dear Service Member,

Thanks for battling the other people. And thank you for trying to get us free. Thank you for caring four our country. Sorry if you cannot go home for the holidays. I bet your family misses you very much. I am sorry if your friends died and you are the only one there. You are very great to all of America. I hope you can go home very much.

Your friend,

Danielle Smith

Oakley, Idaho

Dear service man/woman,

You are the best. Thank you sooo much for EVERYTHING! My family is very thankful for you and so am I. Do you like fighting? I know I wouldn't, but if it meant we would be free forever, I would definitely fight in a war. I wish you the best of luck.

Yours Truly,

Grechen Ainsley Hale

Oakley, Idaho

To Any Service Member:

Thank you so very much for risking your lives to protect us and our nation, and for giving us freedom! We all know how much you are going through; you're going through a really hard time and under a lot of pressure. My uncle Tony is in the war!

We would also like to thank you for giving up many years of your life to serve our country. Things must be very difficult for you men and women! You guys face danger and sacrifices every day! We know you miss being here! We all appreciate what you do, and we hope you can come home and be comforted by your families. We also wish you all luck, and [time] with your families. Hope you can be with your families very soon! Bye!

Your fellow friend,
Makailey
From Murtaugh Elementary
Murtaugh, Idaho

Dear Serviceman,

Thank you for fighting and trying to protect our country. If you are wondering what grade I am, I am 3rd grade. Also, thank you for going to Iraq to fight for our country. If you know what family I am in, the Critchfield's family. Be safe.

Your friend,
Haley
Oakley, Idaho

Dear Soldier,

Thanks for all your fighting for the country that everyone loved and we thank you every day for our freedom.

There's a lot that we could do for our country. You are doing the most bravest thing, so I would like to say thanks for everything.

Sincerely,

Austin Buttars

Burley, Idaho

To any service member,

'Sup, homie? Thank you for your service, dude. That's really cool that you can do something like that. My bro is in Iraq. He likes it. Have fun on your leave.

Peace.

Joshua Bench

Oakley, Idaho

Thank you,

Thank you to those who are fearless. Thank you to those who put on a face of stone every day to save the whole idea that our country is based on—freedom. Thank you for preserving the way of life that we all take for granted. Thank you most of all for being one of the few brave enough to take up this cause.

Taylor

Murtaugh High School

Murtaugh, Idaho

Dear Service Member,

I would like to thank you for the time you've spent fighting. I'm pretty sure it must be hard to be away from your family and friends this holiday. I'm very sure I wouldn't enjoy it. My name is Zachary Carson. I live in Burley, Idaho. I'm seventeen and I live on a farm. I know that sometimes we are forced to do things we really don't want to do. Sometimes we have to do jobs that are difficult or gross, and I want to thank you for that. I want to thank you for risking your life to ensure safety for the people of the United States of America.

Sincerely,

Zachary Carson

Burley, Idaho

Dear service member,

I appreciate all the service you do. I am from Oakley, Idaho. I am in 7th grade. I also have relatives out serving for the U.S. in Iraq. So I feel some of the fear you have. Thank you for everything. Have a merry, merry Christmas!

Love,

Addie Bedke

Oakley, Idaho

Dear service member,

Thanks for saving our country.

From Makinlee

Oakley, Idaho

Dear service member,

I think you for servicing for our country and for the freedom and for me and my family. My dad was in the war but he got sent to the wrong place. He still is a veteran. My gramps, he was a veteran too. Thanks for fighting for our country. I'm going straight to war like my dad but not the same. I'm not getting sent back and getting sent to the wrong place like my dad.

William Wells
Oakley, Idaho

Dear Soldier,

Thank you so much for doing this for our country. You are awesome! I hope you aren't too cold and lonely over Christmas. I REALLY appreciate you (a lot). Thank you so much!

Love,
Laynee
Oakley, Idaho

Dear Soldiers,

Sorry you can't come home for Christmas. I don't even know you and I already like you. I really hope you win the war. If you get this on Christmas, good for you. Merry Christmas! I really hope you have a very good Christmas.

Your friend,
Alexa D.
Age 8-Burley, Idaho

Dear Service Member,

I would just like to take some time and tell you how much I appreciate your service to our country. I cannot even imagine all that you left at home to go into the armed services. The selflessness you displayed is a great example.

Please let me share a small story with you. It was my 8-year-old's turn for prayer. As she was saying the family prayer, she [asked God to] please "bless the soldiers who keep me and my family safe." I have always taught my children to honor the soldiers who keep us safe and to always thank them when they see them in public. So, you can imagine how it touched my heart to hear the most precious thing to me say that. From that day on, you have been in my family's prayers. My family is so grateful for you and your service that we can't even put it into words. May you return to your loved ones. God speed and many blessings. Thank you for keeping me, my family, and this country safe and free.

Thank you,

Tyler Davis

Burley, Idaho

Merry Christmas,

Soldiers, thank you so much. We really appreciate you. You really are wonderful. Love,

Sierra L. Phipps

Declo, Idaho

Dear Soldier,

Our state misses you. When Iraq is free, come home to your families.

Love,
Megan
Santaquin, Utah

Dear Soldier,

How is it there? What day is it there? How many soldiers are there? What time is it there? When do you get to see your families?

Sincerely,
Jayden E.
Juniper, Idaho

Dear Soldier,

My name is Alexus and I want to appreciate you going to Iraq and fighting for our lives. Well, I have an uncle up in Iraq and another in the navy. It's hard not to see them all the time. They say it's worth it. I guess you think it's worth it too, because you are fighting for me and my family too. Well, it's sad not to see your family all the time.

I hope you like my letter later.

Sincerely yours,
Alexus Ochoa
Burley, Idaho

Dear Soldier,

I appreciate what you're doing for the U.S.A. and the people of our country. It makes me feel really good inside. I hope you really like the army. It's nice.

My grandpa was in the Vietnam War, but he died this summer.

Sincerely,
Anthony Cordova
Burley, Idaho

Dear Soldier,

I appreciate what you are doing in Iraq. I was wondering if you like fighting in battle? My name is Mazie. I have a brother, mom and dad. They are great. My grandma was in World War II.

Your new friend,
Mazie Moser
Burley, Idaho

Dear Soldier,

Do you like killing bad guys? What are you doing? Do you have a rocket launcher? Thanks for fighting bad guys. I hope you had fun in Iraq. I think you guys are cool. I would like to be in the army some time. I exercise some times.I hope you are safe.

Sincerely,
Anthony Clayton
Burley, Idaho

Dear Soldier,

I appreciate what you are doing for our country and everybody else. Every time my dad watches the news I hear about people going to Iraq and Germany and sometimes getting killed in other places.

My dad is in the Marines. He has gone to Iraq and fought for the country just like you soldiers. My life is trying to do good in school and hope to try go to college to be just like my dad.

Sincerely,
Duane Johnson
Burley, Idaho

Dear Soldier,

I appreciate you fighting for our freedom. I want to be like one of you who fight for freedom. Be safe, OK? My niece Meyana is going to join with the U.S. Army so they can pay for her college. She can do more than one hundred push-ups.

Please get this letter I write. If Michael Arredondo C. is not there, then one of you can keep this letter. But if you know him, tell him I miss him a lot. I always will, no matter what happens.

My family appreciates what you do for them.

Sincerely,
Selena Ortega
Burley, Idaho

Dear Soldier,

I appreciate what you are doing because of saving the United States of America. Every American should be thankful that our land is free.

Sincerely,
Aaron Linares
Burley, Idaho

Dear Soldier,

I appreciate what you are doing for the people of the United States of America. When I grow up, I want to be a soldier like you guys.

Sincerely to the soldiers,
Jesus
Burley, Idaho

Dear Soldiers,

I thank you for fighting for me and giving me freedom, because if [I] weren't I don't know what I would do.

My teacher had told us that you guys aren't coming home for Christmas. I thought that I'd write you a little letter. That way you wouldn't feel lonely if you didn't have anyone to talk to or spend time with you. You would have a letter from me to read.

Sincerely,
Daniel Evan Smith
Burley, Idaho

Dear Soldier,

I wish we all could be free and be like you soldiers. I appreciate what my family does for their kids, cousins, aunts, uncles. I have an uncle in the U.S. Army. He's learning to fly helicopters. He's the best uncle in the army.

Sincerely,

Bryana Ortega

Burley, Idaho

Dear Soldier,

Thank you for going to war so we can have freedom. Does it get cold [there]? Do you have military time? My uncle was in the army once. My friend has an uncle in the army too.

Sincerely, your friend,

Alexis Nara

Burley, Idaho

Dear Soldier,

I think what you are doing is cool. I wouldn't have the right to be free. I couldn't do just any thing if I wasn't free. For instances, I like to play with my cats. I might not be able to do that.

Sincerely,

Courtney Johnson

Burley, Idaho

Dear Soldier,

I appreciate that you are brave enough to fight for our state, and I hope you win the war in Iraq. When you win the war I will be a solder just like you when I grow up.

If you are wondering who is writing to you, my name is Daniel. I'm a Mexican. Whoever I am writing to, I hope you like my letters. I hope you have wonderful leaders to train you and [be kind to] you while you are training. You will always be in my heart if you lose the war. If you do lose, I will pray for you every day and night.

If you have any children, tell them I said hi. Well, got to go.

Sincerely yours,
Daniel Pedraza
Burley, Idaho

P.S. If you lose, you are still my hero.

Dear Soldier,

I appreciate you for going to war to give me the feelings of freedom. I wish you luck and I have hope in you guys. Stop the war for once and for all. I wish you guys could stop all the men being killed, please.

Please come home forever to see your family. Good luck to all.

Alan Bench
Burley, Idaho

Dear Soldier,

I hope you won't get that cold during the winter. I hope you soldiers will be safe for the winter. All the students here at White Pine School are grateful for you supporting our country. I bet you soldiers miss your family and all the stuff you used to do. If you come upon the Soldier Mr. Beaky, tell him Karsten Hinckley said hello.

I like what you do for the United States of America.

Sincerely,
Karsten Hinckley
Burley, Idaho

Dear Soldier,

I am very thankful for all you have done for us. I appreciate what lives are taken everyday just for us to live.

I am very happy that I can go be anything that I want to be. I am thankful that I can go and do those things thanks to you guys. I hope that you guys are safe in Iraq. It would be a honor to meet you guys. I have three sisters and no brothers. I hope someday to grow up big and strong like you guys. I hope you guys do your job. We all have faith in you, everybody in the U.S.A. does. Just remember that.

Sincerely,
Andre Curiel
Burley, Idaho

Dear Soldier,

I appreciate what you are doing for me and the United States. I wonder how many people are going to fight with you. How old are you? I want to go to Iraq when the war is over.

I am going to Hawaii for Christmas vacation. So don't write me during Christmas vacation. I'm not trying to be rude, but don't because I will be gone.

Sincerely yours,
Shyla Pincock
Burley, Idaho

Dear Soldier,

My name is Randilee and thank you for fighting for our country. If you did not fight for our country we would have to be slaved and beaten to death. Some people do not appreciate what you are doing for them. My grandfather fought in World War II against the [Japanese]. He is still alive today. My other grandma is German. She barely got moved to the U.S.A. before the war started there. I can also speak German. I hope to hear about you when you get this letter.

My dad and my brother like to learn about war. I do, too. I have five brothers and six sisters counting me. Please write me as soon as you get this.

Sincerely,
Randilee Golay
Burley, Idaho

Dear Service Member,

Thank you for making my family safe.

Jessica B
age 5-Oakley, Idaho

Dear Service Member,

We are very happy about what you're doing.
My name is Emily and I am ten.
Merry Christmas!

Love,
Emily
Oakley, Idaho

Dear Service Member,

Hi. I am Daxton. I am so thankful for you. I am six years old. I hope you have a very merry Christmas.

Daxton G.
Oakley, Idaho

Dear Service Member,

My name is Zaden and I am eight years old. I am thankful for you to be a soldier. I am grateful for you to be in the army.

Thank you for serving our country.

Merry Christmas!
Zaden
Oakley, Idaho

Dear Service Member,

I just thought I'd take a moment of well-spent time to express to you my undying gratitude for the hours of selfless service you perform. I strongly admire the remarkable bravery you possess. You bring hope and comfort to people from all parts of the world.

Thank you,

Anna M. (16)

Oakley, Idaho

Dear Service Member,

Happy Holidays! Season Greetings! Merry Christmas!

I hope this letter brightens your season! I am deeply grateful for what you are doing or what you have done for this great country and its people. I'm am so grateful you are brave to be a service man and have to leave your family. That is great courage and bravery. You are doing so much for this country. I'm so thankful for you for fighting for our freedoms, beliefs, ideals, and liberties. You should be proud. I hope you enjoy this Christmas season even though you're away from home.

God bless you! Merry Christmas! Peace on Earth, good will to men!

Chloe W. (15)

Oakley, Idaho

Dear Service Member,

Happy Holidays! Marry Christmas!

Thank you for all the things you're doing for our country. I hope you see your family for Christmas. May the spirit of Christmas be with you.

Aleiha Cranney (11)
Oakley, Idaho

Dear Service Member,

I am sorry you are trapped at an airport in Germany this Christmas season. I am so thankful for your defense of our country, though. Without your service and sacrifice the freedom we enjoy might not exist. Our country would be much more susceptible to disaster and devastation.

I hope you have a merry Christmas and are proud of what you do and have done. Thank you so much.

Justin C.
age 15 - Oakley, Idaho

Dear Soldier,

My name is Domonic. What do you do in your spare time? Will you please tell me your favorite sports and holidays? Will you tell me about your favorite animals and pets you have? Is it hard to be a soldier? It is bad in Iraq? I bet it don't look good. Do you have tanks or trucks or airplanes?

Domonic
Twin Falls, Idaho

Dear Mr. or Mrs. Soldier,

Hi, my name is Ruth Guionnaud. You can call me Elizabeth. I am ten years old. I have four sisters. Their names are Chantel, Christine, Hannah and Elise. Do you have any brothers or sisters? My sisters are annoying. Hannah and Elise were supposed to be boys, but of course they weren't. Did you ever want a brother or sister? My dad is in the air force. Maybe you know Smsgt Rene Guyionnaud. He's my dad. My hobby is singing. Freedom is important to be because the African Americans wouldn't be able to come to school with us.

Yours Truly,
Ruth Guionnaud
Ramstein, Germany

Dear Service Member,

Hi! My name is Andres Loper. I'm eleven and in fifth grade. I have been in Germany for two and a half years. I live with my mom, dad and two younger sisters.

I'm glad that you would [fight] for our country and for our freedom. I hope you have a great flight to wherever you are going.

Best Wishes,
Andrea Loper
Ramstein, Germany

Dear Mr. or Mrs. Soldier,

My name is David Swezey. My age is ten. My favorite sport is football. My favorite card game is Texas Hold 'Em. If you like wrestling, my favorite wrestler is John Cena. My favorite game is Medal of Honor Frontline on PlayStation Two. When I grow up I want to be a Marine.

Enough about me; now for you. What is your favorite sport? Hobbies? How old are you? I wish you a Merry Christmas, and a Happy New Year! I also thank you for what you are doing to save our country and risking your own life for us.

Sincerely,

David Swezey

Ramstein, Germany

Dear Service Member,

My name is Madison Nicole Sumerlin. I am ten and have one brother. My hobbies are swimming, soccer and dance. I have been in Germany one year and two months. School is difficult for me, but I still get OK grades. Freedom is important to me because if you and everybody else in the military were not there we would be getting bombed. Thank you for what you are doing. I appreciate it. Be safe.

Love,

Madison Nicole Sumerlin

Ramsein, Germany

Dear Service Member,

My name is Keondre, but my friends call me Dre. I like to skateboard and [play] video games. I broke my leg skateboarding in the fifth grate. My mom says I can never ride on anything with wheels again. My sister Kaylin can't either. Kaylin is six years old and Kyndal is one year old. I'm the oldest because I'm eleven.

Why is freedom important to me? Freedom is important to me because then I have the right to do whatever I want.

Sincerely,
Keondre
Ramstein, Germany

Dear Service Member:

Ho ho ho and happy holiday cheer!

May the spirit of Christmas be ever so near!

May you have warm and friendly Starbucks, or whatever you please,

Stars, elves, presents, wishes and Christmas trees!

An English teacher wrote this so please don't judge.

Take this silly poem with a wink, a smile or shrug!

Happy holidays to you and with gratitude we say,

Thank you for your sacrifice each and every day!

Sincerely,
Ms. Pristelski
and her Reading Lab classes
at Ramstein High School, Germany

Dear Soldier,

What's your favorite thing to do in your spare time? I've always wanted to be a soldier since I was born and hope I can be one when I grow up. I'm glad that you are defending the United States of America and I hope I will meet you some day in the future.

Sincerely,
Aaron
Twin Falls, Idaho

Dear Soldier,

My name is Claribel Partida. My favorite color is pink and black. My favorite holiday is Christmas because it a family day. In my family there are six people including me. How many people are there in your family? My favorite thing is to color; what is yours? Do you like being a soldier? Do you get scared? Thank all you people for serving our country. If you guys would not be in the U.S.A. Army we would not have what we have now. Have you ever felt like going home or quitting the army? Will you come and spend time with your family this Christmas?

Sincerely, your friend,
Claribel Partida
Twin Falls, Idaho

Dear Soldier,

Hi, my name is Blayz and I was born in New York. I live in Idaho at Twin Falls.

I like Xbox and I have a lot of games. I have over 30 games. I play it almost every day with my brothers. One of them is six and the other one is fifteen. On my spare time I always watch TV for about an hour and go back to work.

I want to thank you for protecting our country and risking your life for us. If I ever meet you, I am going to thank you again for protecting our country all this time.

Sincerely,
Blayz Fischer
Twin Falls, Idaho

Dear Service Member,

Thanks you for fighting for our country and protecting it. We are proud for what you do for us.

Sincerely,
Conner Beck
Oakley, Idaho

Dear Soldier,

My name is Nikolina. I like to work on my math in my spare time. My favorite color is blue. My favorite food is broccoli and my favorite holiday is Christmas, because I get two Christmases. 'Cause I'm from Croatia in Europe. Do you have a family? Do you have pets? What is your favorite thing to do?

Is it fun to be a soldier? You probably will say yes, but you don't want to tell me the truth. That's okay. I know how you feel. Can you tell me why you are a soldier? That would be great. I would give a gift, but I'm not giving this to you by foot. One more thing. Thank you for serving our country. Write back please.

Sincerely,

Nikolina Marcetic

Twin Falls, Idaho

Dear Military Soldier Man,

I hope you get home safe with no wounds.

Chazz

Oakley, Idaho

Dear Soldier,

I hope you are having a fantastic [day], even though you can't see your family. You should know me and a lot of other people in the U.S.A. are very proud of you. You are a colossal help, so don't give up fighting because more than 5 million people need you. I hope this letter touched you, because it touched me.

Thank you for serving our country and bringing peace.

Sincerely,

Makenzie Swafford

Twin Falls, Idaho

Dear Soldier,

I hope you get to see your family. They probably miss you very much and thank you for serving our country and make it safely back home. I don't want you to write back. I am planning to go to the war so one day I will serve our country. I will keep writing you guys. I handle guns because I go hunting a lot. My [favorite] color is camo, I like pizza, my favorite holiday isThanksgiving, I play baseball and I love science. I have two hunting dogs and so just be careful, OK?

Sincerely,
Daniel
Twin Falls, Idaho

Dear Serviceman,

Thank you so much for serving our country. I owe you so much already. I am proud to have people like you that are willing to go and defend what our country is made of.

I wish you the best, and thanks once again for being so brave.

Sincerely,
Kandice K.

Thank you so much for serving our country. Come home safe.

Yasmen C.
Age 6 - Burley, Idaho

Dear Serviceman,

Hey! I would like to thank you for fighting and protecting our country. And to let you know how much we here appreciate you and your fellow comrades. So, keep up the good work and keep safe. Thank you!

Sincerely,
Kyle G.

To Any Service Member,

Thank you for all the good stuff you have done for us. I'm glad I live in a free country. I hope you will be safe. I hope your family will be safe.

God bless you.
Zeke
Murtaugh, Idaho

Dear Serviceman,

Thank you for being so brave to fight for a good cause. I appreciate your service and dedication for this country. I sleep more peacefully knowing you and other men and women are fighting to keep me and my family safe. I appreciate your willingness to leave your family, home and friends.

God Bless America.

Sincerely,
Jessica

Dear Serviceman,

I live in Idaho, and after school every day I go home and work on my dad's farm. I sometimes think that the work I do is hard and painful, but I guess I haven't stopped and thought about the hard work you do. Not only is it hard work, but from what I hear it takes a butt load of courage to fight and protect so many people. I appreciate all that you and all the others with you do for our country. Thank you so much.

Your devoted fan,
Rhett H.

Dear Soldier,

Thank you for fighting for our country. My name is Emma. I feel sad that you can't see your family. When you are in war you risk your life for people you don't even know! Sometimes people think we don't have to fight for freedom. I know that this is very serious. If you accidentally do something wrong in training what happens?

Thanks for fighting for our country.

Emma Lee Coleman
Twin Falls, Idaho

Dear Soldier,

My name is Victoria. What did you like to do when you weren't at war? Do you have kids? Do you really miss your family? I would be sad if I was sent away to go fight in the war. What is it that makes people go to war? I can tell you miss your family members. Are you a girl or a boy? I would really like to know if you know someone called Chris Valdez. If you do, tell her I will miss her very much. I can tell that you are a brave person fighting in the army. I thank you for serving our country.

Sincerely,

Victoria

Twin Falls, Idaho

Dear Servicemen,

I just wanted to tell you that I am very thankful that you serve in our country! I also hope that you are successful in whatever you are doing right now and in everything else.

Laura Z.

P.S. Good luck in your missions and I hope you have a good day. And live your day to the fullest because you never know what is going to happen!

Thank you, military, for helping our country and we're praying that you will come back home and be safe.

Love,

Emilio C. P.

Age 9 - Burley, Idaho

Dear Soldiers,

Thank you for serving our lives. I know you do not know me, but I'm happy USA is safe. I'm in second grade. I'm eight years old. I love books. I have three sisters, and one from one on the way.

Love,

Marie C.

Heyburn, Idaho

Dear Soldier,

You don't even know me, and yet you're risking your life for me.

I'm not sure what I'll accomplish by writing this letter, since no words of mine can possibly express how grateful I am for you and what you are doing for our great country. The reason the United States is so strong today is because of the sacrifices that have been and are being made by courageous patriots like you. Thank you—thank you for your spirit, thank you for your patriotism. Thank you for sacrificing your time and civilian luxuries to serve our country. I appreciate, honor, and salute you. America is the land of the free today because of brave people like you who are willing to risk and sacrifice so much for the greater good.

God Bless you!

Carlie M.

Burley, Idaho

Dear Service Member,

I hope you are OK. I hope you have a good time. I hope Heavenly Father keeps you safe. Be safe.

Sincerely,
Brittany C.

Dear Serviceman/woman serving our awesome country!

Thank you for your selfless sacrifice for all of us. I've never really known anyone in the military—but hey, now I know you! Ha ha! How long have you been serving? Are you in a foreign country? Do you like it? I love writing letters—so if you like writing them too, please keep in touch!

Adelle H.
Paul, Idaho

Dear Soldier,

My name is Lesli. I like to play volleyball in my spare time. My favorite food is tamales. My favorite colors are pink and green. I have a mom, a dad, a brother and two sisters. NO PETS. Do you have a wife? Do you have babies? What's your favorite things to do with your babies? What is it like to be a soldier? Thank you for your time, sir.

Sincerely,
Lesli

Dear Soldier,

The reason why I write you is because I wanted to know many things about you and you should know many things about me. In my opinion I think black and pink are some outstanding colors. My number-one favorite hobby is tennis, and my favorite subject is science and social studies. During my spare time I finish homework and do chores for my allowance. Surely, I would love to read about your life, so may I please ask you questions? What's your name? Do you have a wife or husband? Do you have children? To your opinion, what do you enjoy about the career you have? Without you and your troops fighting for our country, we wouldn't dress the way we want nor look the way we want. Being able to do all these things is incredible. Thank you. Everyone in the world supports you men and women for all you're trying to do for us. In conclusion, thank you for everything you have done.

Sincerely,
Cinthia S.

Dear Soldier,

Hi, my name is Tyler. Do you have any brothers or sisters? Do you have any children? How many children do you have? Also, do you have any pets? What kinds of things do you like to do when you're not busy doing work? Do you like to read or write letters to your family? What is it like to be a soldier? It is harder or easy being a soldier? Do you like being a soldier or would you rather be something else? I just wanted to say thank you for serving our country.

Sincerely,
Tyler H.

Dear Soldier,

Are you married and do you have children? How old are you? What is your favorite thing to do? How is it like to be a soldier and do you like it? Do you get scared when you are about to go through a war? Have you ever been injured seriously? Thank you for serving our country.

Sincerely,
Lesimar

Dear Serviceman,

Thank you for all that you do in the armed forces to defend our country. I appreciate all that you are doing to serve the great United States. I am thankful for your courage and hard work that you do. You are very well appreciated by all who know what you are doing. Once again, thank you for all you do.

Sincerely,
Hailie S.

Dear Soldier,

Hello my name is Eva. . . . Do you love your job as a soldier? If I may ask, is it hard to be away from your family? Can you tell me what your [favorite things] are? What do you do besides fighting? It must be very hard being a soldier. I just want to tell you thank you so much for what you do for our country and for everyone in the United States. If you are ever upset you can always write back and I would enjoy reading about your life. Thank you so much again.

Yours truly,
Eva M.

Dear Soldier,

My name is Kolby. In my spare time I like to build Legos and do the PlayStation. My favorite color is pink. My family, compared to others I've known, are very nice. Do you miss your family? Do you like video games? Do you like being a soldier? If you could go to any place for a military mission where would you go? What kind of metals do military soldiers get for certain things? When you go to boot camp what kind of school do you go to to be a military officer? What time do soldiers have to get up? How strict are the sergeants?

Sincerely,
Kolby

Dear Soldier,

My name is Katryna. I like to baby-sit in my spare time because I love kids. My favorite colors are purple, black and silver. My favorite school subjects are literacy and social studies because my teachers are really nice. My favorite food is deer sticks and salami, but they don't taste any different that regular salami. My family is strange, but I can live with them. I have three snotty brothers. They are 5, 9, and 13. My parents are divorced but they get along better. I have no sisters so that makes me sad. What is your family like? I am sure they are proud of you for defending our country, but are still sad you are not with them. What are some of the things you like to do? Do you like to fish or dance?

Do you ever reject going to the war or not? Are you ever afraid of being injured, because if you are, just remember I'm here and I am proud of you for defending our country. What is it like to be a soldier? I am sure it is really scary, but still I would love to defend my country.

Anyway, I am very proud of you for volunteering. I would love it if you could come home to see your family. I hope to meet another kind soldier because they make me so happy. I hope you liked my letter.

Sincerely,

Katryna M.

Dear Service Member,

Thank you so much for you selfless service for our country. I know how hard it must be to leave your family and loved ones but just remember that you are the one person who makes a big difference in the world we live in today. Thank you again and may God be with you this day and always. Good luck.

Laura H.

Dear Serviceman,

I would like to take this opportunity to thank you for all that you are doing to protect me, my family, and America. It is you and others like you that make me proud of my country. I hope that all goes well for you. Thank you so much for all the sacrifices that you make in your life for me.

Douglas H.

Dear Soldier,

I would like to say thank you for all your courage. It probably isn't easy to go to a strange place and defend your country. It is people like you that help keep this world a safe place. Your service is very much appreciated by a lot of people. Thank you very much for protecting what you believe, because you choose to do it; you weren't forced to.

Yours truly,
Kait B.

Dear Serviceman,

I am from a little town called Malta, Idaho. A lot of people overlook us, but I want to let you know that I appreciate you soldiers very much. I know this letter isn't much, but I hope it means something to you. Good luck and thank you again for all the courageous work that you do.

Thank you.
Ty S.

Dear Service Man,

I am currently a senior at high school. I want to thank you for everything that you have done for our country and it takes a lot of heart and courage to do what you do. You are a hero to me in my book. I just want you to know that I'm grateful for all you have done and all the hard work you have done for are country. Thank you for everything.

Sincerely yours,
A student at Raft River High

Dear Servicemen,

Thanks for all that you are doing. I know I couldn't do it. Thanks for keeping our country free and out of harm's way. Hope you are safe and free from accident.

Blaine P.

Hey,

My name is Tallie. I just wanted to say thanks for everything you've done for our country. I don't know who you are or what you've done in the military, but the fact that you're there representing our nation says a lot about who you are and what you believe in. I don't know if you're really high up in the military or not, or if you feel like you even make a difference. But I believe that everybody out there is important, and that everyone's talents and abilities contribute to our cause and to the goals you've set out to accomplish. So no matter what your standing is, I would like to thank you for the service you have rendered to this country, and the example you have been to me and so many other Americans who look up to you so much. Thank you.

Tallie

Dear Service Man,

Thank you for serving our country. I really appreciate all the selfless time you have spent protecting and serving our country. I would really like to thank all the soldiers who have taken time out of their personal lives to protect the U.S. Thanks again! We love and appreciate you!

A high school senior

Dear Servicemen,

Hello, my name is Brodee. I am writing you a letter because I want to tell you how grateful I am for you. It's men like you that make it so we can live in this country. I appreciate all of the hard work you do for our people. To tell you a little about myself, I like to work. I have had a job since I was eight. I think to make a good man he must know self-discipline and gratitude. Something means more if you do it yourself than someone else doing it for you. I like to play football and be with my friends. I live in a country where I enjoy freedom. Well, thank you again. You're the man.

Sincerely,
Brodee

Dear Soldier,

My name is Tanner. My grandpa fought in World War II, so I really appreciate what all of you do. I am in 8th grade, I love basketball, volleyball and video games. In fact, one day I hope to be a video game designer/ tester. Again, I'm so thankful for all you do, and I think you are so courageous. Well, thanks again.

Sincerely,
Tanner T.

Dear Serviceman,

I appreciate all the hard work and dedication you give to our country. I can't even begin to comprehend all that you must give up to fight for our country. It takes a lot of bravery and courage to do what you do. For that, I, along with my peers, give unto you our sincere appreciation!

Katie B.

Dear Serviceman,

Hey! I felt like I just had to write to say that I am grateful for all that you are doing for me. You're putting your life on the line for mine. I don't think I have ever done anything as selfless and brave. I know that a letter doesn't say thank you nearly enough, but thank you. Thank you for keeping me and my family safe. I hope you stay safe and I will be praying for you every night. I know you have loved ones that you wish you could see again. I pray that you will. Thanks for everything.

Steven D.

Dear Serviceman,

Thank you so much for all you do for us so we can have freedom. I really appreciate all you do. It means a lot. I am so grateful for all of you that have enough courage to do what you do! Hope everything is well.

Thanks again,
Lindsay H.

Dear Serviceman or Servicewoman,

I would just like to tell you how much I appreciate the sacrifices you are making right now in protecting our country. I have no idea what you are going through every day, but I just want you to know that the people back home still love you and want to make sure that you are safe. Your safety is always in my prayers. I know that some people are against the war and that lack of support would probably disappoint most people, but, just remember that most of the people here are trying to support you wonderful people in the protection of the greatest country in the world. I have nothing but respect for every man and woman out protecting me and my family. Just remember that you are doing what is right. Those people need you there in Iraq. Thank you. I can never repay you for what you are sacrificing right now being away from your family, but I just offer you my appreciation and my friendship. Thank you so much.

Sincerely,
Todd Z.

Thank you for being in the army and helping our country for us. I hope you have a Merry Christmas. Is it cold in Iraq? I want you to have a good time.

Sincerely,
Missy

Dear Serviceman,

Hey, hey!!! How's it going? Well, I hope great! Thanks so much for fighting for our country! I look up to everyone that's willing to fight for me, my family and friends. That's freakin' awesome that you have the courage to do that. Once again, thank you! You have no idea how much everyone thanks you and is grateful for your strength and courage. I am a young lady that can enjoy hanging out with my friends and family and not worry about anyone interrupting it. I feel safe that you are out defending our country!

Thank you!

Sincerely, your friend,
Braneli

Dear Serviceperson.

My name is Dallas, age 14 from Malta, Idaho. I am writing this to let you know how much I appreciate the things that you do to help our country and for the cause of freedom. My goal is to be a doctor and work at Shriners Hospital for Children and help other doctors. I hope you come back safely.

Dallas

Dear Serviceman,

Thank you for the service you are performing for our country. I don't know if you hear that a lot or never, but I honestly do appreciate all that you do for our country. I am a 10th grader. I play sports, usual stuff that high school kids do. I love reading, watching movies. I love living in the country and being able to enjoy all of its perks. I am so thankful that you serve so that I can enjoy these things and so can others everywhere.

Again, thank you for all you do.

Sincerely,
Marli

Dear Soldiers from Bryce,

I hope you have a good time in Iraq. I am writing this because I think you guys are doing a good job over there, so keep it up. Thank you for doing a good job. I think you guys are great because you guys are saving our lives. So thank you.

Dear Servicemen;

Hey! My name is Cody. I am writing you to tell you thank you for your service and all that you do. Because you put your lives on the line to protect my freedom, along with millions of others, means a great deal to me, as it does to everyone else in this wonderful nation. So thank you for all that you do and I wish you a safe return home.

Thanks again,

Cody P.

Dear Service Person,

My name is Delani. I am from Malta, Idaho, a little town. I am in the 8th grade. I have blue eyes and blond hair. Both of my parents are teachers out here. Our school is writing letters to soldiers. You are the lucky one, and get to read mine.

First, I would like to day how grateful I am that you would be so altruistic. Many people would not take the opportunity you have to volunteer for our country. My dad was also in the military when he was younger.

Secondly, I hope you can fulfill all of your life's dreams, goals, and ambitions. Some of my life goals are to graduate, go to med school and get married and have five kids. If you have any kids, I hope that you are safe for them.

I would just like to say thanks again for serving our country. Because of you, I can feel safe at night. Thanks for all you do and for all of your hard work and effort. Please know that my prayers are with you.

Sincerely,
Denali M.

Dear Service Member,

Hi, my name is Keely and I'm from the little ol' town of Almo, Idaho. I am 16 years old and a junior. My school is really, really, REALLY small. There are nineteen kids in my grade and about 100 in the whole high school. I really like going to a small school.

I love working on the ranch that my family lives on and riding horses. . . . I also love to clog. (And no, it's not a plumbing problem, if that's what you were thinking.) If you don't know what clogging is, it's just like tap dance but a lot faster and with some extra taps on the bottom of the shoes. I was able to travel to Taiwan and Bulgaria with my clogging team these past few summers and it was an amazing experience. It has really opened my eyes and made me appreciate all that I have here in the good old U. S. of A. I am really thankful for all that I have. I hope that you're able to say the same thing about yourself.

I think that it is really neat that you are willing to put your life on the line to help our country. My cousin just got back from fighting in Iraq a year ago. He went and drove the tankers down there. He served his time and we were all glad to have him come home. I hope that everything goes OK for you and that you will be safe. I hope the war will be over soon. Whenever I think of war, the song "Letters from Home" by John Michael Montgomery always pops into my head. Thank you so much for all that you do! People really appreciate it. I hope you know that you and all the troops are in my prayers. I hope everything goes well for you, and the letters from home keep you going strong. Remember to pray when things get too tough.

Love,

Keely W.

Dear Soldier,

Hi. I'm in the fifth grade and I have four brothers and I am the only girl. I would like to tell you that I know that you helped make our country free. How many kids do you have? Are you married? Have you ever had or have friends in the war? What branch are you in? I would like to tell you that I know you keep our country free. I know you're working as hard as you can. I know fighting in Iraq is hard, but you still work your hardest. Please write me back. Thanks.

Beth C.

Dear Serviceman,

My name is Reagan. I would just like to let you know how much I appreciate your bravery and courageous acts for our country. You are symbols of America and its heroes. I hope you remember when you're in Iraq that you have people here that are supporting and thinking about you.

Sincerely,
Reagan W.

Dear Serviceman,

Because of your faithful service I am able to attend my rural high school and enjoy the freedoms that are protected by loyal people such as yourself. The world is much in debt to people like yourself and those who are willing to give their lives for the benefit of others. Your example is seen through many representatives and patriotic themes around the nation. Because of you, our flag will fly those colors bolder, the people walk taller, and attitudes will turn to gratitude and selflessness. I appreciate the service given in past years, now and years to come! I send a huge thank you.

Thank you!
Jayme M.

Dear Service Man or Women,

All I have to say is thank you for risking your life for our country America. To me you're a hero. Thank you.

Please write me back.

Sincerely,
Dakoda

Dear Service Person,

Thank you so much. You mean a lot to me and others. It's near Christmas. I'm excited. I hope you are too. Have a holly jolly Christmas. I wish you the best of luck. Words can't describe how much you're helping. Thank you so much. May the angels be watching over you on this special night.

Love,
Taryn W.
5th Grader

Dear Soldier,

Today we are celebrating Veterans Day. Thank you for going out to battle so we can be free. You are being really brave and having a lot of courage. Thank you for your service and freedom for us. I hope that you see your family soon. Thank you so much for risking your life for us and hard work. I wish you good luck. I hope you and other soldiers have won the battles.

Sincerely,
Jordyn Greco

To Any Service Member,

Hi! My name is Zac. I am a fifth grader. Thank you for risking your lives to protect us and our freedom, for giving up those painful years of your lives to protect us and our freedom. Thank you for serving in the military and for serving our country.

Sincerely,
Zac Bean

Dear Soldier,

Hi, I'm Justin and I'm ten years old. I'm in the fifth grade. How old are you? I'm guessing 42 years old. How many guns are in the army?

Your friend,
Justin

Dear Veterans,

Thank you for the prize you gave me for the coloring contest. I took my time and colored very carefully because I was proud of this wonderful country. Each one of you is a true hero the way I see it. I want you to know I am so grateful for my freedom and life here. Once again, thank you for my prize and thank you for all you did.

Sincerely,
Sarah Sanderson

To Any Service Member,

Hi, my name is Bernice Orozco. I am in the 5th grade. I am from Mexico and I come all the way to Murtaugh, Idaho. Thank you for risking your lives to protect us and our freedom and giving up years of your life to serve in the military and for serving the country.

We hope you come back safe and can be with your family again. We know you are under a lot of pressure. You face danger every day. I know you miss being here. You probably miss the comforts and freedom you have here. We appreciate all of the sacrifices. You make our lives good and our country free.

Thank you.

Sincerely,
Bernice

Dear Service Member,

Thank you for defending our country and making it free, and giving me the right to be free. I appreciate what you've done and hope you get some time off.

Yours truly,

Devon Andersen

P.S. Both my grandfathers were Army men on boats.

Dear Service Man,

My name is Mallory. Thank you for serving our country and just a few days ago was Veterans Day, also known as Armistice Day. We had a Veterans Day program and all the parts in it involved World War I and World War II. We recited about 30 parts/paragraphs about people who served in the armed forces or just plain fighting. After that we had a moment of silence. All of us today thought of you and all the armed forces or just troops.

Be safe in Iraq or whatever you are doing. Hope you have happy holidays, like Thanksgiving and Christmas coming up. Merry Christmas! Happy Easter! (etc., etc.) Thank you so much. Keep up the good work in serving our country. Be safe!

There is one bright star in the deep, dark sky. Look at it closely, and it will guide your life.

Your friend,

Mallory Critchfield

Dear Service Man/Woman

Are you having fun? I bet it is hard there. I hope you have a good one.

Yours truly,

Shayna Lierman

Dear service member,

Thank you for defending our country. Stay alive.

From,

Mitch

Dear Soldier,

My name is Angel. Thank you for serving our country. My dad is in S.C. basic training. He will go to Iraq. What is Iraq like? I'm going to send food for soldiers. That way they won't have to eat MREs.

Sincerely,

Angel

I am so grateful for such wonderful people like you! I wish I could meet you and tell you of my appreciation for your service. What an extraordinary person you must be. Have courage knowing you are loved and cherished as a service member and wonderful person known as an individual and so appreciated.

Love,

Jordan Manning

Dear Soldier,

My name is William and I am ten years old. I have one brother. I am in 5th grade and my parents got divorced four months ago. I have moved six times and have been in two schools. I have never really been able to get along with anybody, so I mostly make enemies more than friends, but that was at my old school. But I still have trouble getting along with a few people at my new school, but not so much anymore. Have you ever been shot or shot at? What part of the military do you work in? Do you miss your family at all while you're away from them? It is frightening getting shot at when you don't even know?

Sincerely,
William

Dear Serviceperson,

I send my greetings and thanks to you for your work to defend our country. May good fortune smile upon you. Thank you for everything you have done, not only for me, but for all of America. I wait for the day when every single serviceman and servicewoman will be able to return. Thanks again for your protection.

Cody Muhlstein

P.S. Many people have difficulties pronouncing my last name. (It's Mule-steen.)

To Whoever Receives This Letter,

I'd like to express my gratitude towards you and the many soldiers who are willing to fight for our country. Thank you deeply. I wish that there were many more who share our views so that more of us can truly enjoy our freedom.

Andrea Anderson

Dear Service Member,

I appreciate all the service you do. I am in the 7th grade. I also have relatives out serving for the U.S. in Iraq. So I feel some of the fear you have. Thank you for everything.

Love,
Addie Bedke

Dear Soldier,

Hi, my name is Terry. I am a boy and I am in the 5th grade. I'm ten years old. I was wondering if you had any kids. I am very glad that you guys are defending our country. I am glad that we don't have to live under the rules of another country. What I'm trying to say is keep up the good work! Let the other countries know that America is going to be free forever!

Sincerely,
Terry

P.S. Are you scared to be in the Army?

Dear Soldier,

Thank you so much for doing this for our country. You are awesome! I hope you aren't too cold and lonely. I really appreciate you a lot. Thank you so much.

Love,
Laynee

Dear Serviceman,

We are all very proud of you for defending our country. My uncle recently came home from serving. Please be very careful.

Your friend,
Whitney

Dear Service Person,

I am taking a minute to say I really appreciate what you are doing. Thank you for your service and dedication to our country. I really cannot express in words what I feel for the sacrifices you are making for all of us at home. Our prayers are with you always. I hope everything with you gets sorted out, where you're at, so you can come home.

Thank you again for all you are doing and what you stand for.

Sincerely yours,
T. Gonzalez

Dear Service Man/Woman,

My name is Jacque Bench. My brother is in Iraq fighting and I hope you like it as much as he does! I think you are really great to be able to leave this country and go fight for it! Thank you so much for being brave enough to do that.

Sincerely,
Jacque Bench

Dear Soldier,

I hope you now how much this country loves you and how much it appreciated your sacrifice and unselfish acts. We owe our carefree lives to courageous people like you. I really hope all goes your way. Thanks again!

Josh Anderson

Dear Soldier,

Today we are celebrating Veterans Day. How many days until you go home? I really want to see what it is like there. Thank you for your hard work.

If you don't have beds like we do what do you sleep on? How many years are you there? I hope you see your family soon.

Your friend,
Kylie Jo Robinson

Dear Soldier,

So, how are you? How is Iraq? Thank you for fighting for our freedom! Is the army hard? I hope you get to see your family soon. What time is it? Well, where are you? Well, I want to grow up to be like you! To fight for freedom! Thank you for freedom! I hope you get to see your family soon.

From your friend,
Wade Evenson

Dear Service Man/Woman,

Thank you so for serving for our country. I pray every day for you. I love living in a free country. I love it so much that I can not explain it. Again, thank you.

Yours truly,
Kelsey Martin

Dear Service Person,

Thank you for fighting in the war. I think you are great person. Thank you for helping us be free and I hope you can send us a letter back. I hope you can come and visit us someday. I hope you are okay and happy. Once again, thank you all.

Love,
4th Grader Racio

Dear Service Member,

Thank you for what you are doing. My name is William. My favorite animal is a dog. What is yours? Do you have a hobby? I have many like reading, cooking and playing sports. How long have you been in Germany? I have been here two years, almost three.

What rank are you? Be safe! Have a great flight! You make my day doing what you do.

From,

Tom

Ramstein, Germany

Dear Service Member,

Thank you! Words can't express what you have done for us, so I won't even try. Thank you isn't even close enough to sum it up, but it's the best I could do. I'm only in seventh grade and I can't save the world, but you can! You are amazing! I know that you can't be with your family this Christmas but we want you to know that while you are thinking of your family this Christmas that a whole (very thankful) nation is thinking about you.

Love,

Janel Peterson

Oakley, Idaho

Dear Soldier,

Thank you for what you do. I am ten years old. My name is Adam. My hobbies are making things, playing outside and playing Xbox.

What are your hobbies? Where are you going to or where did you come from? If you're going somewhere I hope you have a good flight. I hope you have a Merry Christmas.

Freedom is important to me because if we didn't have freedom our country would be horrible and we wouldn't have a say in anything. That is why freedom is important to me.

Sincerely,
Adam
Ramstein, Germany

Dear Service Member,

My name is Alaina. I am ten years old. I have brown eyes and brown curly hair. I'm in 5th grade and I go to the Ramstein Intermediate School. My favorite sports are baseball and football. My hobbies are scootering and drawing. What are your hobbies? I hope you are safe. I have been in Germany for almost one year. Thank you for what you are doing for our country. I think freedom is important because it keeps us together.

Sincerely,
Alaina Hensley
Ramstein, Germany

Dear Service Member,

I wanted to share my thanks and gratitude for the great sacrifice you are making in behalf of our nation. Both of my grandfathers, as well as my father, served in the Armed Forces, and the sacrifices they made for America have created a wonderful sense of patriotism throughout our extended family. I hope that your service is creating the same type of loyalty to our country within your own family.

Thanks again,
Chad Daybell
Springville, Utah

Dear Soldier,

We salute you and we honor you for the sacrifices you and your family are making to help the millions of Americans who depend on you for their safety, freedom and way of life. We are an active-duty military family stationed here in Germany and faced with upcoming deployments of our own. It is hard to be away from family and friends for any amount of time. It is especially hard to be gone during holidays, birthdays, anniversaries, births and other special occasions. We have been there, and we understand the sacrifices you are making.

It is a sacrifice to serve in the military. It is a sacrifice to go off to war. And above all, it is a sacrifice to be willing to lay down your life for freedom and for your fellowman.

My family is patriotic to the core, with red, white and blue running through our veins, and we pray that just maybe this letter of encouragement and support will offer you a piece of mind, a ray of hope and a smile to your face that might not otherwise be there.

Please know we support you, we love you and we pray for you on a daily basis. My three-year-old little girl always thanks her Father in Heaven "for the Soldiers that love me." We echo the sentiment, for it is love for your family, your country and your God that you serve. Please know that we support you and we love you.

Lift up your head and be of good cheer; this too shall pass and you will be a stronger individual than ever before, if you endure this trial well. The Lord has great things in store for you if you will be faithful and valiant, and when you return home, know that your fellow countrymen will be waiting, with open arms, to welcome you back.

Love,

Joe, Tawny and Ceilidha Campbell

Landstuhl, Germany

Dear Service Person,

Thank you for fighting in the war. You must be a great person. I'll be cheering for you. Thank you for helping us be free.

Riley

Dear Service Member,

Wherever the holiday has placed you, please know you are never alone. We are a proud nation and realize that freedom isn't free—it never has been. I am a 55-year-old army vet, my husband a retired Special Forces commander. We live in Southern Idaho and have a son in Iraq. He serves with the 297 Infantry, a guard unit from Alaska. Like you, we have spent many holidays away from family, many in remote areas. There are times when I look in the mirror and say, "Did I really do all those things and live through it?" Yet, always knowing I did. You have only to ask for guidance and it will come, but you must ask. Thank you sincerely for your contribution to the safety of our country. Bless you in your travels.

Edna Pehrson
Burley, Idaho

To Any Service Member,

It is a privilege to write you. I was raised in a patriotic family—my father served in WWII. Each time I see the flag, I get those goose bumps and am forever grateful for the sacrifices of your service in continuing to provide the protection and freedoms that I enjoy.

I live in rural Idaho. Each day I breathe fresh air, listen to chirping birds, watch the moon come up and see beautiful sunsets. I listen to rippling water and enjoy the smell of fresh-cut hay. I have a safe home for shelter and a church close by with freedom to worship as I choose. I do not have to run for cover.

I had the privilege of a good education (I am a nurse). My children have a great appreciation for the flag and the freedom they enjoy. They are grateful for the men and women who serve our country. They in turn are serving in their communities, helping to improve others' lives. We are all able to do these things because of the brave men and women who are [defending] and have defended truth and right. Thank you.

Jolene Robinson
Burley, Idaho

Dear Service Person,

It is the holiday season and I would like to let you know how much America appreciates you. It is really nice knowing that there are people such as yourself out there continuously working to protect the freedom we have today and enjoy. I am at the age that if the draft were reinstated, I would be drafted into the service. I am so very grateful that there are those who work and give me the opportunity to pursue my college education instead of going into the service after high school. This is the holiday season and we know that sometimes service people aren't able to see their families during this time of year. We greatly appreciate the sacrifice that you are making to secure our freedom and our opportunities to see our families when we want to.

As a Thanksgiving family tradition, we go to my grandma's cabin in Riggins and stay there as we go elk hunting in the Riggins area with black powder guns. This is a family event because my older siblings that are moved out come and spend Thanksgiving together as a huge family with parents, grandparents and nieces and a nephew sharing this wonderful time.

I hope that you hold and treasure memories like these and that when you're able to see your families again that you will be able to make new memories that you will be able to enjoy later.

Tyler Payne
Burley, Idaho

Dear Serviceman,

Greetings from the great State of Idaho! Snow is currently on the ground here. The roads are icy. You might wonder why the preoccupation with the weather. We are Americans raised in Canada and winter driving there is dangerous. We as a family and individually pray for your safety. We also pray for your families and the sacrifice that each and every one of you makes. It is very difficult to be separated from families at the Christmas season. We appreciate your sacrifice.

We will never forget the sight of seeing the World Trade Towers coming down. It is difficult to understand that kind of hatred. But, we believe in the love of an Eternal Father who loves each of His children. This more [than] any time of the year is felt by the outward deeds of goodness that is manifested all around daily. Last year, my oldest boy made an ornament at a children's church activity. As we were leaving the building a four-year-old girl dropped and broke hers. Seth, seeing her tears, said, "Here, take mine." Our Savior was once asked, "Who is our brother?" You are our brother. How grateful we are to live in a land of freedom, that we may choose to educate our children how we desire.

May the spirit of the season embrace you in the warmth of the Savior's love. Remember the King who was born as a babe in a stable, who gave all so that we might return and live with our Heavenly Father.

Love,
The Spackman Family

Dear Soldier,

My name is Aldo. I am writing a letter to you in Iraq. I just want to say God bless you and thank you fighting for our country, not ours but yours. You guys earn lots of love, so I'm writing that you guys are sweet enough to earn freedom. It's hard for you guys to fight this war and just let God in your hearts and strength to get this war to an end.

But thank you for fighting [for] what we want to say, wear, what games we want to play, and so thank you, thank you for everything you done and to all you soldiers, pioneers, heroes.

I'll always think of you guys who are in Iraq, so I'll always cry American tears for you guys.

God Bless You.

Sincerely,
Aldo Tello
Twin Falls, Idaho

Dear Service Member,

At this holiday season, we reflect upon the blessings we enjoy. One of those blessings is you. You have set aside your personal matters to give unselfish service to your country. We want you to know that your effort and service do not go unnoticed.

May your heart be warmed knowing that we appreciate your giving of your time and talents for the great cause of freedom that we all hold so Dear. We do not ever want to take it for granted.

Thank you.

With much love and affection,
The Koyle Family
Heyburn, Idaho

Dear Special Person (anywhere there is a lonely serviceman),

You are probably servicing not because you want to, but because you have been asked. Thank you for your sacrifice and your bravery. We hope that this note will brighten your day a little bit. We live in Idaho where it is winter now, cold and snowy. We are thankful for the freedom that we have in our great country. This is protected by dedicated people like yourself. We hope that the little bag that has been prepared for you will bring a little cheer to you on this Christmas Day. [The] homemade cookies . . . might not be just like your mom's, but they are meant to try to be like hers in a small way. Thanks again and Merry Christmas and may the coming year be a blessed time for you. May our Father in Heaven bless and protect you and your family.

Love from Idaho.
Melvin and Enetta Call
Burley, Idaho

Dear Service Member,

For some time I've wanted to write a note of appreciation like this. I didn't because I wasn't sure what to do with it after it was written. So this is a joy to me to get to express my gratitude.

Whoever you are, thank you so much! Last fall at a craft fair I saw a plaque that read "Land of the Free Because of the Brave." That has got me to thinking, for you are brave. Especially so in an all-volunteer army, navy, air force, marines, Special Forces, Green Berets, and the wonderful rest of you. Thank you so much for defending America!

I'm not sure whether this is to be a short note or it can be a lengthy letter. I know it will be read before it gets to you.

In the town where I live, my neighbor was a navy

man. We watched his wife raise their five children pretty much alone. He would come home maybe three to four times a year for a week. Those little kids needed their dad so much that they just seemed to absorb their father's personality. They became so much like him! They needed him so badly! It was then that I noted the sacrifice. He eventually retired and one 4th of July he spoke to our religious congregation and left us with this poem. I immediately wrote it in my journal and have since tried to memorize it.

Freedom has a price
And always, it is high
Sometimes a man must give all he can
Sometimes a man must die
And give away all his tomorrows
To those of a future day
Who never understand the sorrows
And the price that someone had to pay

Please believe that I do have gratitude for your sacrifice. You are making a difference in the battle between good and evil. What we do in this life does echo through eternity. I do believe in a higher power and this constitution and land is a choice gift from him.

Sure, America has its problems. Our politicians are mostly corrupt and seem to be arm chair generals. Those people are not necessarily heartland America.

Heartland America does believe in you. We believe you are doing the best you can in spite of the politics.

My heart goes out to our veterans. I vote, speak well of you, salute you when you walk past in parades, I admire you in uniform from a distance, chills run up my back when I hear your service anthems sung. I try to be a good citizen and I don't litter America. I have a flag that I fly on holidays and sometimes when I just feel patriotic. I've taught my three sons it is an honor to serve. I would support them, if they should be drafted, that they should serve this land with love. I believe in a God, a just God that will balance every injustice in the end and will balance the scales in the end. He'll make everything fair and heal all wounds. Believe in the God of this land. Always keep your integrity, no matter what. Do the best you can, that is all you can do. You will be all right in the end.

May your soul be protected. May your family be protected. May you feel the love people have for you this Christmas season. I've included some brand new Hallmark ornaments. I love Hallmark stuff. I wanted you to have the very best. Nothing used for you, only new. Have you heard Lee Greenwood's song "God Bless the USA"? It's a favorite of mine. The next time you her it, think of this letter. That rendition will be to you from me.

Love,

A 50-year-old American Mom
from Idaho

To Any Service Member,

Thank you for your sacrifice of time and for your service to our country. There is no way to pay you back for that which you risk to keep our country safe and free. The dangers you face and the comforts you give up for the sake of freedom and your country are not in vain. We honor and appreciate you, and pray for you continually.

May God bless you through the difficult times and bring you home safe and sound. You are in our hearts and minds and prayers. Thank you.

Sandy Seever
Murtaugh, Idaho

Dear Service Member,

Thank you! Thank you! Thank you! You are so awesome. I am indeed grateful for your sacrifice. We are blessed to live in such a fine country.

You are wonderful in my eyes and I am so grateful for people like you. I would never have the courage to do what you do.

I really appreciate your sacrifice you make for me and our great country. It really takes courage to put forth your life for people you don't know.

You are amazing. Anyone who puts their life on the line for what they believe in is a true hero. Keep up the good work. Thank you! Thank you! Thank you!

Braden
Burley, Idaho

To Any Service Member,

I just wanted you to know that the personal and family sacrifices you are making are appreciated here at home. I have had members of my family serve in nearly every branch of the military. My daughter is a navy recruit.

I am grateful for all you do and for all that those who have gone before have done to keep the world better for those of us here at home.

Be safe,

Deb Cutler

Murtaugh, Idaho

Dear Service Person,

I am writing this letter not only to wish you a Merry Christmas but also to thank you for being where you are and doing what you are doing at this time. I feel it is a privilege to be writing this note because of the sacrifice you are making. I thank you from the depths of my heart.

Sincerely yours,

Gib Hunter

Oakley, Idaho

Dear Service Man or Woman,

As our family gathers together every Monday evening, we [take] a moment to thank those who put themselves in harm's way to keep us safe and ensure our liberty our forefathers sacrificed so much for. We pray for your welfare and safety every night. We think of you often, especially when I place my hand over my heart and renew my allegiance to my God, my country and family. May God bless you and protect you. I pray your burdens may be eased and you are able to support this huge responsibility placed on your shoulders. Thank you again.

Our Lord and Savior once said, blessed is he who lays (or is willing to lay) down his life for another. He finds eternal life in doing so.

Again, may God bless you and your loved ones as you are away from home.

Sincerely,
David Critchfield
Oakley, Idaho

Dear Service Member,

My son-in-law is a Marine and has served in the Gulf and various other places around the world. It is so hard for family at home and I know you who serve miss home, especially during the holidays. I am proud to be associated with anyone who is willing to serve our country by defending our freedom against despots. Know that you are thought of and prayed for often. Thank you for serving your country.

A Proud American
Oakley, Idaho

Dear Patriot,

Thank you for your service to our great country. I believe God has a special place in his heart for brave men and women who stand for liberty and justice. May you be protected always. God Bless You!

My kindest regards,
Dennis Smith
Oakley, Idaho

Dear Serviceman,

I am thinking of you today and want you to know you are appreciated and respected by Americans everywhere. I live here in Columbus, Georgia, and know something about what you are going through because I talk with other young men who are stationed here at Fort Benning. I know you have been through a lot to be trained, prepared and dedicated to the cause of the military. What you are doing to defend freedom and the liberty of all people is at the heart of what we in America are all about—the right to live in a country where we are truly free to become the best we can be. I want to thank you for all you are doing to help this happen.

I have a family of six children that we have raised here in Georgia. I know family life is the greatest happiness I have, and I am thankful for the blessings of living in this free country. To be able to raise our children in a land where law and order are fair and just, to be free to work and serve here in our community, to have the opportunity to worship as we believe, these are great freedoms. You help to make these freedoms possible and I thank you for all you are doing.

I know the Lord will watch over you and protect you as you pray to Him and strive to live a righteous life. I am grateful for the Savior of the world and His great commitment to mankind as He atoned for our sins and made it possible for us to gain our eternal salvation. At this Christmas time may we always remember Him and seek to follow in the path He has shown us.

Please know again that you are loved and appreciated.

Best of Wishes to you,
Valeni Witbeck
Columbus, Georgia

Dear American Soldier,

I know you are far from home and your loved ones, and that is on my behalf. Thank you! I appreciate your service to our country and your efforts to help us remain free and safe as a nation. I also want you to know that you are in our family prayers every morning. We pray for your safety and direction in your duties. Thank you so much, and I hope your fond thoughts of family and friends will sustain you while you are far away from your home and family.

Bev Ramsey
Burley, Idaho

Our family wants to let you know how thankful we are for your service and sacrifice for your country. We know how hard it is to be away from home, friends and family. We hope that this helps to lift your spirits and put a smile on your face! May God bless you.

Sincerely,

The Radicic Family

West Point, New York

Our family is thinking of you with hearts full of gratitude for the selfless service you give. We appreciate your willingness to serve our country. May this holiday season bring you comfort and a sure knowledge that your efforts are making a positive difference.

Best wishes,

Mark, Shaunna, Luciano and Paolo Tonelli

West Point, New York

Dear Service Member,

During this holiday season, we wish you joy, hope and comfort. May your life and service to our country not be forgotten and may you be blessed continually with all you need. Thank you.

The Campbell Family

West Point, New York

USMA

To Any Service Member,

I live in a little town in Iowa with my husband and seven-month-old baby boy. This holiday season really makes me reflect and realize how blessed I am, and you are one of the reasons I am blessed. You are making a great sacrifice so I have safety and freedom to enjoy.

It must be difficult to be so far from loved ones. I pray for them and for you. I am so grateful for what you are doing.

Love,

The Helm Family

Kalona, Iowa

Dear Service Member,

Just a note of thanks for your service in protecting this goodly land and for the sacrifice you are making, that we might still enjoy the freedom we still enjoy. I love this land and it makes my heart swell with pride to see Old Glory flying, to know that you are striving to keep it this way.

Wishing you, and all who are in the service of our country, a Merry Christmas and hope the conflict will soon be over. Thanks for everything you are doing to preserve our freedom in this goodly land.

Venola Archibald

86 years young

Oakley, Idaho

To Any Soldier,

Thank you for fighting to keep our country safe and to make life better in other countries. We know you are sacrificing a lot and we are grateful.

The Sparrow Family
West Point, New York

To Whomever Receives This Letter,

Your devotion and service on all our behalves is acknowledged and very much appreciated. You may not hear this as much as you should, but that doesn't diminish the importance of what you do. I hope your family and friends are also proud of you. My prayers are with you this day and I hope you travel in safety.

Kerry Anderson
Rupert, Idaho

Dear Service Member,

On this Christmas Day, I want to thank you. You are away from home, friends, family and especially you are away from a traditional Christmas. I know it has got to be hard to be away from everything familiar on a day like this. I can't pretend to know what you're going through, as I am a stay-at-home mom with three kids and one on the way.

As I sit warmed by the fireplace I find myself wishing I knew who I am writing to. I look around at the beautiful tree, the decorations hung on the wall and the dazzling lights and I wish I could share them with you. I would love to know your name, home, religion, traditions, etc. Then I could make this even more personal. As it is, I don't know you and we'll probably never meet. But I hope that in some small way, I have helped to brighten this day for you.

I am so grateful for the sacrifice that you have made for your country. I know it's hard to be away from everything, but I want you to know that there are people back home that love and care for you. I have two brothers-in-law in the army, so I know what it's like for them to be away during the holidays. I know your family loves and misses you.

You are always in my prayers. May the Good Lord watch over and protect you and bring you home safely.

Erin Hansen
Hansen, Idaho

Dear Service Member,

As we come to this Christmas season, we all think about what is really important in our lives: wives, children, mothers, fathers, friends, religion, freedom and our country. You are out there protecting all of these as a member of the Armed Forces. It matters not if you are in the navy, army, marines or any of the other defenses that guard against the evils of the world. You have volunteered, not been drafted or pushed, to serve your family and your country in a special way.

You will be away from all of these special things

and your families during this Christmas. I know what it is like to be away from home and loved ones during Christmas time, and I hope this letter will brighten your day and spirits.

I want you to also know how much your service to this country means to me. It means freedom to do. It means safety at home. It means my family is safe because you decided to protect us from harm's way. I appreciate your sacrifice on my behalf. I love you for your dedication and hard work. I will always remember you for your courage and love of this country.

Remember always that God is in everything and that putting your trust in Him will always bring you to where you will want to be in the end. Walk in faith and know that I and my family are praying for you. Keep your ears alert, your heart open and your head down. Your families want you home and so do I.

Nolan Hansen
Hansen, Idaho

Hi,

We want to thank you for your dedication and service to our America. Our appreciation for what you have done and are doing, no words can express how we feel. You have given much and given up much. Thank you,

You are in our hearts and prayers.

Allen and Patty Butler
Burley, Idaho

Dear Friend,

I can call you friend even though I don't know you. You are my friend because you are doing something for me that I can't do for myself, which means an awful lot to me. You are defending me, mine and the country that I love so very dearly. Thank you so much for your sacrifice at this time in your life.

I sincerely hope that this day will be a little brighter for you.

Thank you again for your efforts!

Sincerely,

A lady from southern Idaho

It is such a great blessing to live in a free country. Our history is rich with many who sacrifice as you are for democracy and freedom.

Thank you so much for carrying on the tradition and cause we all believe so deeply in.

May God bless you for what you are doing in representing our way of life, our constitution, our heritage and our families.

I have a son who is with you somewhere. Keep up the good work.

Sincerely,

Stan Campbell

Juniper, Idaho

Dear Soldier of our Armed Forces,

We just want you to know how much we appreciate what you are doing for us here in America. We pray for our soldiers in every branch of the service every night. We hope you will be encouraged by knowing so many people love you and are thankful for what you are for each and every one of us. May God bless and protect you.

With much thanks,
The Wagemans
Burley, Idaho

Merry Christmas,

I am not sure whose hands this letter will end up in, but I do know if you are receiving it that you are not able to be home with your family during the holidays. I know from personal experience how lonely it can be to be away from family and friends this time of year, but know in your heart how proud they are of the work you do. You are protecting our right to live free and helping others to realize that dream. I, myself, look up to and admire you and all the others who have answered the call to serve, 'cause that is something I will never be able to do.

I was born with ataxic cerebral palsy, which is the mildest form of the disability. So, I still walk with a limp. If there is one thing I have learned it is not to take anything for granted. I may not be able to follow in your brave footsteps, but I can look at the flag with pride and know that because of you, and the other people, before and after you, I can lay my head down and sleep, knowing what the flag stands for. I can stand proud and know I am free to celebrate with family and friends in a country where the only limit is the one I put on myself. I hope by writing this letter I can bring a smile to you during the holidays.

Thank you for all you do every day and know you will be in my prayers. Thank you for allowing me to be a part of your holiday.

Sincerely yours,
Ron Conner
Burley, Idaho

Hi,

We as a family are meeting in the safety of our small community in our church to celebrate Christmas. We have so much to be grateful for. As we go about our lives we do not forget you and your great sacrifice. My father served in WWII and my son is in the army. My father lost his life. May the Lord be with you and protect you so you can return to your family and friends.

We pray for you and your family daily.

A mom who cares
Juniper, Idaho

To Any Service Member,

Words alone can't thank you enough for the service you are giving to our country—to individuals—to me.

Thank you for your courage, concern and sacrifices so that others can live better lives. May God bless and protect you.

Sincerely,
Marci Larsen

Dear Soldier,

Thank you! Your sacrifice to serve us has not gone unnoticed by me, and never will. I couldn't imagine having to leave all that I know behind to go to fight and not know if I were ever gonna come back. It's noble and I am thankful to you for it. I thank my Heavenly Father every day for soldiers like you. I also pray for your safety.

Take care,
Ruth Weaver
Cedar Fort, Utah

Dear Armed Services Person,

Just a brief letter to extend a huge THANK YOU for your service to our country. A letter seems inadequate to express my deep gratitude for all you do. At this special time of year, I wish you a Merry Christmas. My thoughts and prayers are with you during this wonderful season.

My family prays for you every day, and I am teaching my three little ones to love and respect our flag, our great country and especially our brave and honorable soldiers. We support you during this crucial war on terror. Best wishes and thank you for being a true hero. God bless you.

Melissa Davids
Burley, Idaho

Dear Service Member,

I truly hope you realize how special you are, and what an important service you are providing, to not only the United States, but to everyone in the world seeking freedom from oppression. I am grateful for your willingness to take the time and make the sacrifice to serve in the Armed Forces, and to be away from both family and friends. I hope that all this time, during the Christmas season, that maybe this letter and the other gifts you get will help to make a lonely time a little bit brighter.

I spent six years in the army in the early 1970s and can really appreciate what you are doing and how lonely it can be during the holidays.

It is really neat to see the support there is, not only here in southern Idaho, but all over the country for all the work and sacrifices you make.

Thank you and may God watch over you always.

Ray C. Archibald
Oakley, Idaho

To Our Dear Servicemen and Women, Our Heroes,

Our thanks and prayers are with you in your righteous endeavors. My dad was a pilot in the air force—test pilot on F14s—spent 3 years away from his family—1 year in Korea in the '50s—and 1965 and 1967 in Vietnam. He is 86 years old now and retired near Eglin AFB, FLA—and he'd be over there with you now if they'd let him and walks 4 miles a day briskly, golfs three times a week. I got to live at Hahn AFB when I was 2 and again when I was 13 and 14—loved it.

I work at an alternative school and we often have recruiters in to inspire the kids to greater heights. We so appreciate your sacrifice and want you to know we support you, and you, of all people, know the good you are doing for the oppressed nations of the world. Let freedom ring, and may peace and comfort and the comforter be with you always. God is watching you.

Merry Christmas and a hope-filled New Year

Rex and Anne Martin
Oakley, Idaho

Greetings to you from cold and snowy Idaho,

It has been 45 years since my husband and I spent our first Christmas in Fort Leonard Wood, Missouri, where he was stationed with the 144th Evacuation Hospital during the duration of the Berlin Wall Crisis. We didn't make it to Germany, as some units did.

We value and appreciate the blessing of living in

America and thank those of you who are serving to safeguard all she stands for.

May the spirit of the season bring peace to your soul and to the world.

Thank you for your service.

Jerry and Celia Marchant
Oakley, Idaho

Dear Service Member,

We don't know each other but my heart goes out to you this Christmas season.

I'm retired from the military as of three years ago, so I'm aware of the feelings of being in transit during this season of the year.

My family lives in Oakley, Idaho and our wishes and prayers are with you and your family at Christmas time.

We appreciate the good work you are involved, and the sacrifices you make, for not only our freedom [but] for the freedom of all those who are oppressed throughout the world. I know your family is sacrificing a lot in your absence also.

May God bless and protect you as you continue to serve this great nation.

Sincerely and with respect,
Jerry Wells and family
Oakley, Idaho

Dear Servicemen,

I sincerely hope your weather there is warmer than here. I checked the temperature gauge tonight and it's 21 degrees. I was happy to have the opportunity to write to you. I hope your holidays are treating you well. I have a high respect for you for serving our country. Every time the national anthem is sung or the flag is raised I always take that time to think of our precious troops overseas.

My prayers are with you and your families. May the Lord bless you and your endeavors. I'm sure you're looking forward to going home. Just remember—we're pulling for you in the States!

With lots of love and encouragement,

Tonya R.
Oakley, Idaho

So it seems not-so-personal to be writing to no one in particular. I am at a church Christmas social and they asked us to write a letter to a serviceman. Certainly sounds like a noble cause and so may I express my thanks to you for fighting for freedom. While I enjoy watching my children color a picture in the warmth and comfort of a church here in a peaceful state, you are living amongst turmoil and the sounds of war.

May I just tell you that you and people like you are what makes America good. Regardless of what the media may portray to you, there is a father and mother of five beautiful children from southern Idaho who are grateful for the cause you stand for. May God in Heaven bless you with protection that you may return home to find that all is well. May He bless your family at home with peace and love and great satisfaction to know they have someone who is boldly defending freedom. Have a wonderful time with what you have this Christmas, even if that may only be the memories of what has been and will be.

Sincerely,
The David H. family
Oakley, Idaho

Hi Servicemen!

I hope you are all fine. We live in Oakley, Idaho. . . . We are three hours from Boise, Idaho and three hours from Salt Lake City, Utah. The weather is cold and snowy. I am writing to you because I appreciate all the servicemen, especially what they do for our country! My husband was in the Vietnam War and that was bad enough. We have four kids, two boys and two girls. May the Lord bless you through the coming year. I wish you a Merry Christmas and a Happy New Year. I hope you that you will see your family soon.

Sincerely,
Jerry R.
Oakley, Idaho

Dear Service Member,

Of all the things in this world that mean the most to me, it is freedom that ranks at the top. We are a very blessed people to live in the United States of America, a land saved and preserved for a people to live free. I have enjoyed this freedom all of my life and until I first left the United States some years ago, I did not realize just how precious my freedom was. My life has been different since then, and I have gained a deeper understanding of how much freedom really costs.

With that said, I must personally thank you for risking your own life for me. Whenever I hear of the loss of any soldier, my heart goes out to their family and loved ones. I wish I could have been with that soldier to help or save. So my love and support and prayers are for you and your safety as you faithfully serve this country and the world. You are important to me! Please come home safe.

Denny Davis
Oakley, Idaho

Dear Service Member.

I would like to tell you how thankful I am for you and for all that you do for our country. Our freedoms that we so enjoy are made possible by all of the hard work and sacrifices that you make. I hope you have a Merry Christmas. I hope you make it to your destination and have a good time.

A friend from Oakley, Idaho

Dear Service Member,

We are so very grateful for the service and sacrifice you are giving for us and our country! At this season we tend to think about all that we're grateful for. With all that is happening around the world these days, you rank very high on our list!

We pray for your safety and for your families left behind!

God Bless You!

The Koziol family
Oakley, Idaho

Dear Service Member,

I wanted to take this opportunity to thank you for your sacrifice for our country.

Our two sons are both in Iraq serving in the Army Reserves so we know how hard it is to leave your family.

Everyone comes up to us and tells us that they are praying for all of the military service members serving, so you are remembered.

I will continue to pray for your safety.

Carol Bedke
Oakley, Idaho

Dear Service Member,

I want to take this opportunity to express my appreciation to you for the sacrifices you are making to serve our great country! Being away from family and loved ones is never easy—but especially difficult at Christmas. I am proud of all those who volunteer their services in the protection of the freedoms we enjoy.

The support for the military we have witnessed is great and plentiful. Hundreds have been more than willing to help Ian Archibald with this project of his to provide a little Christmas for you and so many others who are also away from home in the service of our country.

May you feel our love and that of our Father in Heaven. He knows you and is aware of all that you are going through.

We pray for your safety and may you and your family feel the peace of the season.

Love,

Ray and Cheri A.
Oakley, Idaho

Dear Service Member,

I am proud to be an American. The national anthem always brings tears to my eyes.

Thank you for being willing to serve our country and keep it safe.

May thoughts of family and home bring you joy this Christmas season.

Pam Jenks
Oakley, Idaho

Dear Service Member,

Warm holiday wishes from Oakley, Idaho! This holiday season is much like many others, a light dusting of snow and evening temperatures in the single digits—brrr! Our hope is that you have a merry holiday season and have the opportunity to spend it with friends.

Please accept our sincerest gratitude for your service on our behalf and behalf of our country! We hope that the many prayers offered for you each day will bless you this season!

Greeting with affection,
David D.
Oakley, Idaho

Dear U.S.A. Service Member,

Just a quick note of support and greetings of Merry Christmas from Idaho! We are so grateful and glad you do what you do—no matter what the crappy media says, the Lord and most of us are behind you all the way!!!

We sure live in the greatest land of all and we have you personally to thank for that! May the Lord return you home soon and safe.

Ginger J.
Oakley, Idaho

Dear U.S. Service Member,

Just a quick note to tell you how much I appreciate your service. We live in the greatest country on earth. However, I also realize that this blessing comes at great cost. We have been able to enjoy this blessing because of men and women like you who are willing to give of their time. At this Christmas season when you are away from your family please know that mine prays for you. I am so thankful for your willingness to serve so that my children can enjoy the blessings they do. We pray for a quick end to this conflict.

Merry Christmas.

Forever Grateful,
Michelle Marchant
Oakley, Idaho

Dear Service Member,

Merry Christmas! I know that it must be hard for you to be away from home for Christmas. I have two family members that just got home from Iraq. May the Spirit of Christmas bless your heart that you may know how many are thinking of you while you serve overseas.

We are so proud of each of you that are risking your lives to serve your country. I am grateful to you and those that serve with you. I support you and feel you are fighting for a good and noble cause. I quote a few lines from our own Declaration of Independence, "Prudence, indeed, will dictate that Governments long established should not be changed for light and transient causes; and accordingly all experience hath shown that mankind are more disposed to suffer, while evils are sufferable than to right themselves by abolishing the forms to which they are accustomed. But when a long train of abuses and usurpations... reduce them under Despotism, it is their right, it is their duty, to throw off such government, and to provide new guards for their future security." That is what you are trying to do, "provide new Guards" for the Iraqis' future security. May the good Lord bless you and protect you from harm. May you have a very Merry Christmas.

Thank you,
Ryan Cranney
Oakley, Idaho

Dear Service Member,

As I write to you I enjoy the freedoms you protect. You stand for freedom, justice, and all the people who are safe because of your service. I've never met you, I've never seen you, but I'm proud of you. Thank you for standing up for our country. I'm sorry you're stuck in the airport, but I know you'll make the best of it.

Sincerely,
Jonathan Hale
Oakley, Idaho

Dear Military Person,

We want you to know how proud we are that you are choosing to serve your country and want you to know that we are very thankful that you are fighting for our freedom.

Please remember the reason for this season, the birth of our Savior and Redeemer Jesus Christ. Know that He loves you. Your family and friends love you and we are all praying that the Lord will continue to protect you from harm's way.

We wish you a very Merry Christmas and hope that this will help to brighten your day.

We also wish for health and strength for the coming New Year.

God Bless You!

Lorna A.
Oakley, Idaho

I would like to tell you how much I appreciate all that you do for our country and my family! I am a mother of three boys and you help to keep us safe!

Come home soon and know that we support your efforts 100 percent.

Thank you.
Heather W.
Oakley, Idaho

Dear Service Member,

Here's a little note with a big wish for you at this Christmas time. It is my wish that you may know how grateful I am for your service to our country, wherever that may be.

I am so grateful for your service to us as individuals as well as our country. I pray for your continued safety and health wherever you may go next. Whether home or overseas, may you always know you are not far from our hearts. And as you go forward this day, may the Lord bless you now and in the future.

God bless you,
Janna E.
Oakley, Idaho

Just a short note to let you know you are not alone on this Christmas. People in the small community of Burley, Idaho, have you in our thoughts and prayers not just during the Christmas Season but every day.

Please know what you are doing is very much appreciated and our support is with you and all that are currently serving.

May you be blessed this day and may your heart be filled with love and peace, if only for a little while.

Merry Christmas.

Karlene B.
Oakley, Idaho

Dear Beloved Serviceman,

[I know] you are far from home right now but I wish you a Merry Christmas and your loved ones, [and] also all those that are traveling with you. Our heartfelt thanks to you for serving our country so far away. . . . I'm sure your having been where you have been has made a difference in many lives. I wish we could hear what you have been through.

God bless you and your family. If you ever come to Idaho you will be welcome here. Come enjoy fishing, skiing, hunting, camping, etc. I hope your future is a good one for you and your loved ones.

Thank you for all you do. May God protect you always.

Elizabeth D.
Oakley, Idaho

Just a note to let you know how much we appreciate everything you are doing to make America safe and keep our freedoms. Thank you for all of your sacrifices that have been made by you and your family, parents, wife and children. It must be very hard for you all, especially at this time of year, but know we pray for your safety and think of you often.

What you are doing is not being done in vain. We will stay free and unafraid to sleep at night. We know this because we know God will not let our country fall. You are part of that and keep faith that He is watching over your loved ones.

To the service people, you who put your lives on the line each day in preserving our precious liberty and freedoms—a great big THANK YOU.

At this special Christmas Season may God watch over you and keep you safe from harm according to His will.

You all are so much appreciated for your service.

It's difficult for me to really express what I feel in my heart for your sacrifice.

May God bless you and yours.

Sincerely,

Don and Adyta G.
Oakley, Idaho

Dear Service Man or Lady,

They tell me you are in Germany. I wasn't in the service but I was in Germany as an air force civilian working for the government. I had a grand time over there for four years. The service clubs are very nice—make good use of them. My husband was a Senior Master Sergeant—one of the first to get that rank.

Have a great time while there but hurry home and enjoy the freedom over here.

Merry Christmas to all of you and may God bless you.

Florence W.
87 years old
Oakley, Idaho

At this Christmas time, we are reminded of the land we love and those who keep us safe and free.

Thank you from the bottom of our collective hearts for your service to our nation and to each and every one of us.

We are doing our best to teach the youth of the sacrifices you are making and the cost of freedom to each of us.

Thank you again for all you do. Our collective thoughts and prayers are always with you.

God bless you and God bless America.

Keith Ramsey
Burley, Idaho

Dear Service Men and Women,

I would like to say thank you for putting your family aside to put your life on the line for the U.S.A. I think about you often and pray that God keeps you safe. Even though it seems that the war is a downer, it is all for a good cause. Please never feel that you want to give up. In the end you can say the verse in the bible, "I have fought a good fight and I kept the faith!" GOD BLESS YOU AND STAY SAFE ON THE FRONT LINE.

Olivia P.
Burley, Idaho

Dear Service Men (or Women),

I wish to let you know how much my family and I appreciate what you are doing to preserve the freedom of our great country. I sincerely hope your tour of duty is successful and that you will come back to us safe and in good health.

My family is rejoicing the fact that my grandson, Jason L., just returned from his tour in Kuwait. It's so good to have him back. He has three more years of duty so he may see more action. Each day I pray for all our service people, both men and women.

I'm sure our God will be with you and all those who share the job you are all doing.

I'm an 81-year-old "Gramma" and will pray for you, the receiver of this letter, for a long time.

Thank you again for what you are doing for all of us.

Love and prayers,
"Gramma" Clara
Burley, Idaho

Dear Soldier,

Just a note to say thanks from the bottom of my heart for all you are doing for our country!

Only those who have served as you are can know how difficult your job is or the satisfaction of doing something for the good old U.S.

My Dad served in World War II and I remember his tales of sudden danger, close escapes, crazy escapades, and cold, wet nights. The thing he wanted to be remembered for after his death was that service.

I wish you a Merry Christmas and Happy New Year. I hope in some small way this Christmas will be unforgettable. As I pray for peace, I'll pray for you, too.

Blessings,
Linda
Burley, Idaho

Dearest Serviceman or Servicewoman,

Thank you from the bottom of my heart for the part you play in protecting all Americans and helping others secure their freedom. You wouldn't be where you are if you didn't feel that freedom is a very special thing. I hope you have family that love and miss you. The job you do is an important one, one that most Americans love you for and wish you a safe journey home. I have a son that just got out of the marines. He wants to serve more but his heart says no (medical). I wish you a speedy and safe return home to family and friends, Thank you, thank you, thank you. We all love you.

We fly the flag for you every day!

Darla G.
Burley, Idaho

To a Special Serviceman,

This is just a special Christmas greeting to express our appreciation and gratitude for your service to us and our country. We know how difficult it is under any circumstances, but especially at this time of year. It's not much of a replacement for it, but please accept our heartfelt thanks and our love for your sacrifice. If you're ever in Rupert, Idaho, look us up—we'd love to make your acquaintance and thank you personally.

Page C.
Burley, Idaho

Dear Service Person,

We really take our hats off to you for your love and service for our great country. Thank you so much for your sacrifice and dedication, putting your life on the line for all of us here at home.

I have a nephew serving in the army. He is stationed there in Germany. He just recently arrived there from Baghdad. We hope he will still be able to return back to the states. His family lives in Utah. His name (just in the slightest chance you know him) is Scott Price.

May the dear Lord bless you. We wish you a very Merry Christmas and a Happy New Year. Thank you from the bottom of my heart. I pray you might soon be home with your family and loved ones.

Sincerely with love,
Delores G.
Burley, Idaho

Dear Service Person,

I would just like to tell you that I am so thankful that you are over there fighting for this great country of ours. And that is just what it is today because of you guys over there. I just want to tell you all how much I appreciate you. I just want to stress I love you guys for what you guys are doing, for your bravery [and] loyalty, because that is just the words and many, many more that describe you guys. Well, I could just go on forever.

With lots of love and
appreciation,
Tiffany A.
Burley, Idaho

Hello and Merry Christmas to you from our family in Oakley, Idaho.

We hope as you make your way to wherever you are going this day that the peace and serenity of our Savior's love may abide in your heart and may you find happiness in knowing that there are those of us here at home who believe in what you are doing. We revere you for your selfless sacrifice; we honor you for your bravery. We respect you for your dedication. We pray for your safety and security and for your loved ones there at home.

Because my husband had a military career, personally we understand what gives you the fortitude to carry on and do the work of an American patriot.

Please know that this Christmas season we are thinking about all of you who are fighting for the cause of peace throughout the world, for freedom from terrorism.

May this Christmas season give you a feeling of peace, love and happiness.

Renee Wells
Oakley, Idaho

To Any Service Member,

I would just like to say that you are my hero for serving this wonderful country. I hope that you can enjoy your time without the comfort of your home and loved ones. I encourage you to stay strong, though I don't know of the trials you have gone through. Please know that you rock. Again, I must say you are my hero. Allow me to say I hope that you may know that there are people out there that care for you. Hopefully this letter may touch you or some other service person reading over your shoulder in a way that can only be reached through words. Thought I may not be able to send you a gift, I hope this will suffice.

Please know that there are people out there that would give almost anything just to be able to thank you for your services, large or small. Service is service and I thank you for that.

Sincerely,
Hunter Wadsworth
Oakley, Idaho

Dear Service Person,

I am sure you are missing the holidays with those special people back home, and it must be a very difficult time for you. But I hope you know the importance of your sacrifice for those of us here.

Freedom is precious, and we can be thankful because we are free to gather together and worship (or not), we are able to express our beliefs (or not). Freedom is a precious gift and we are thankful to you and all veterans for representing us in that fight.

I believe you are true heroes. As Americans we tend to hold up the famous, the beautiful and the rich as heroes. But our real heroes are the faceless men and women who fight for our liberty, who love this country and who will sacrifice their time, miss their families and risk their lives so we can continue to celebrate what's important to us.

Thank you.

May God richly bless you, your family and your unit today and tomorrow.

B. M.
Burley, Idaho

Dear Service Person,

I do not know you, but your sacrifice will bless me. I have not met you, but I know what you fight for will somehow make a difference in my life. You are faceless to me, yet because of you I am free! Free to celebrate, free to gather, free to worship. I am truly blessed to live in a nation where I am not hungry, I am not poor, and I am warm and blessed beyond other nations. I know that God has placed brave and courageous men and women to protect our freedoms. Thank you for standing for freedom. Thank you for your sacrifice. May God richly bless you and your family during the holidays. You are not there for nothing. You are there to make the world a better place.

Merry Christmas.

Thank you that I continue to celebrate our Lord's birth!

Barb
Burley, Idaho

Dear Service Member,

We don't know each other and probably will never meet, but I want you to know that you and all of our troops are in our hearts and prayers each day. Your bravery and strength of character represent what America stands for. You portray what we Americans value most—freedom. The U.S.A. is the "land of the free and the home of the brave," but only because of the courageous people like you. Each of you plays such an important role in protecting our country. Please always remember what you are doing will always be appreciated and never forgotten.

Thank you for your commitment and bravery. May this letter help bring you good health, clarity of mind and the courage you need. I cannot find the words to express how grateful I am that you're putting yourself in harm's way to protect our way of life. It hits close to home as my fiancé is serving in Korea right now and will be spending his Christmas alone. I wish you and your fellow service members complete safety throughout your tour of duty. Please know that we are behind your efforts and appreciate you. You are all heroes to me! I wish you all the best and pray for your safe and speedy return home to your family and friends. May you return to a true hero's welcome!

Sincerely,
A grateful supporter!
Burley, Idaho

Dear Service Person,

On behalf of the Board of Directors, the staff and the seniors we serve, we would like to send holiday greetings to you. Many of our members are veterans and can appreciate your service to our country. They too know how difficult it can be to be in a strange land among different people, customs, etc. We thank you for your sacrifice and dedication to this country. We believe that you are very special. May God bless you, your unit and your family. And we hope you and yours have a wonderful Christmas filled with blessings today and to come.

Rupert Senior Center
Rupert, Idaho

A Happy Holiday Greeting:

First off we would like to thank you for serving your country and protecting our freedoms. We pray each day for all of you to return home safely. We have a nephew who is currently serving in the U.S. Navy.

We are a retired couple of "seniors" who recently moved from Pocatello to Rupert, Idaho. We are enjoying retirement—keeping busy camping, fishing and rodeoing.

We have family scattered in the western states—so many places to visit and twelve grandchildren and one great-grandchild to enjoy. We are kids at heart, decorating extensively with three Christmas trees. [We are] currently working on our outside nativity scene.

I hope this finds you safe and please know you are loved and appreciated.

Sincerely,

Janet and Vic B.

Burley, Idaho

Dear Soldier,

I am very sorry that you are away from your family at this time of year. Your dedication to the United States of America is unbelievable. You'll always be loved far and wide for the sacrifices you make every day. I live in Germany away from most of [my] family so I understand somewhat of what you are going through. It is very sad not being able to have a traditional holiday with family and friends everywhere, but I hope you know how thankful we are that you do what you do. America is truly behind you. I volunteer at Landstuhl Hospital and every time more injured soldiers arrive, almost the whole hospital goes out and helps them get to each place in the hospital they need to go. Even though you are not with your family right now, I hope you feel how truly loved and grateful America is to have you giving up your holiday for us. There might not be a lot of holiday cheer where you are, but I hope this brings you some. I will probably never meet you, but I wish I could be with you right now. I know how important it is to be with loved ones at this time, and I hope you get to them soon. Be safe and thank you.

Cassie Lindsey
Ramstein, Germany

Dear Soldier,

Being stuck away from home and family must be hard. At times you probably feel like giving up. But don't worry because there's people out there that care for you and realize how hard it is. Never give up because in the future it can only get better. It won't be too long till the war ends. Someday there will be peace and we can all celebrate and forget about hard times.

Good luck.
Garth
Ramstein, Germany

Dear American Soldier,

As I think about the holiday time I reflect about love and family. I wanted to take the time to express my appreciation for the sacrifices you have made. I realize how difficult it is being away from family for such a long time. I am stationed overseas as a DoDDS teacher and find being away from close friends and family quite challenging at times. However, not only do you sacrifice your time away from them, but you also risk your life day to day. Your courage and honor are immensely appreciated.

When I am having a terrible day and think that my personal life is in shambles, my students don't care about reading and doing their homework, and that life is too hard, I start to feel guilty. How could I compare the trials of my life when yours take such a larger precedence?

I know perhaps you face many questions from those who may not support your cause. I have heard many questions from those who may not support your cause. I have heard many active duty members state, "I'm just doing my job." Please know there are many who support you and care. You are doing a job that most would not be willing to take on. May you have peace and happiness throughout this holiday season and throughout your life-long journey.

Best wishes always,

Tiffany

Ramstein, Germany

Dear Soldier,

I can only imagine how hard it is to spend your holidays away from the people you love. I only know how it feels to have my Dad deployed during the Christmas season. No matter what is said about the negative images being shown by the media, know that what you do for our country and others is greatly received and appreciated. While spending this time away from your family is not enjoyable, I hope that you know that the people living in the Kaiserslautern Military Community are grateful for what you do. . . . [I want] to let you know how much I value what you do and know that your family will be there waiting for you to get back and see them. If you are injured I hope that your wounds heal quickly and you can be back up on your feet dancing the night away when you return home.

Sincerely,
Allan Miller
Ramstein, Germany

Dear Service Member,

Hi, I work in Washington, DC, and I live in Vienna, Virginia. I have had many friends and colleagues who have been in the military. My husband was in the navy (Desert Storm/Desert Shield). I think he was LUCKY—he came back safely and the fighting was really brief.

I am very, very grateful for your service and

sacrifice. We in the U.S. are so lucky to have someone like you protecting us. We should never forget how difficult your job is and how great the sacrifice you and your family must make. I hope that you are able to come home to your friends and family safely and that you do not have a difficult time readjusting.

If you ever get lonely and want to write and receive some e-mails, please contact me. Please be safe and take care of yourself. Come home soon!

Love,

Karen

Washington, D.C.

Dear Service Member:

I don't know if you are going to or coming from, but my heart and prayers are with you at this special time of the year. I am a retired serviceman as of three years ago, so I know how it feels to be in "transit" at this time of year.

My family and I live in Oakley, Idaho. We wish you a very merry Christmas and thank you for the sacrifices you make for us and all the other nations who are seeking peace. We also wish a special holiday for your family, as I know how much they have to sacrifice in your absence. May God bless and protect you as you continue to serve this great nation.

Sincerely,

Jerry Wells and Family

Oakley, Idaho

Dear American Soldier,

I can't fathom what you are going through at this time. However, I wanted to take a few moments to let you know many people care about you, including myself. During this holiday season, I know it is challenging being away from family and friends. While I have been living overseas, I realized how I miss out on many opportunities to spend time with loved ones. Nevertheless, I also know I have a responsibility to fulfill. Thank you for your courage, dedication and sacrifice.

I thought I would share one of my favorite poems that my gymnastics coach gave to me. The poem reminds me to stay positive in times of struggle.

The tree that never had to fight
For sun and sky and air and light,
But stood out in the open plain
And always got its share of rain,
Never became a forest king
But lived and died a scrubby thing.
The man who never had to toil
To gain and farm his patch of soil,
Who never had to win his share
Of sun and sky and light and air,
Never become a manly man
But lived and died as he began.
Good timber does not grow with ease,
The stronger wind, the stronger tree.
The further sky, the greater length.

The more the storm, the more the strength.
By sun and cold, by rain and snow,
In threes and men good timbers grow.
Where thickest lies the forest growth
We find the patriarchs of both.
And they hold counsel with the stars
Whose broken branches show the scars
Of many winds and much of strife
This is the common law of life.

- Unknown

Hope this holiday season brings you peace, warmth and happiness!

Best Wishes.
Tiffany
Ramstein, Germany

Dear Service Person,

I want to thank you for standing on the wall—protecting our country. I know what it's like to be away from home and family and I admire you for what you are doing and you chose to volunteer to protect our country.

I served in Vietnam and I understand some of the feelings you are going through.

Please keep up the good work and if you are in Iraq, please keep your head down and gun clean.

God bless you and keep you safe.

Carl C.
USN (SS) Ret.

Dear Serviceman and Woman,

While everyone is home with their families this year enjoying good company, your season has been dimmed being away from family and home. I want you to know how much it means to me for what you do. You're sacrificing your holiday to support the entire world, which is an extraordinary gift. Never forget that your nation supports you and is eternally proud for what you do every day. As a student living overseas most of my life, I understand how depressing it can be to be separated from family at the most important of times. So while you're waiting, remember that your family and nation are PROUD of everything that you do for this nation.

Tristian
Ramstein, Germany

Dear Service Member,

I wanted to take a moment to thank you from the bottom of my heart for the sacrifice you have made for our great nation. I can't express what it means to have the security I feel for myself and my family. I don't fear for our safety and that is due to people such as yourself.

Growing up in a military family, I know all about the countless hours/days/years that you spend away from those you love. Please know that no matter what, you have a place reserved in my heart along with countless others whom you have never met. Please continue to serve well. We pray health and safety in the selfless service you provide.

Please consider this a long-distance hug from across the world.

Your friend,
Rochelle Schoenborn
Washougal, Washington

Dear Serviceperson,

In appreciation for what you are doing and what you have done for us, [the] U. S. of America. We are so grateful for your service.

Hope things with you are going well. Things all over are questionable, but with faith in you people and faith in the Lord above, we will be taken care of.

May the Lord bless you with your needs,
Lois L.

Dear Service Member,

Our family would like to express our appreciation for the choice you have made to serve in the military, especially during these trying times! We, too, are a military-minded family. My husband served in the army during the Vietnam War era and currently two sons-in-law are active duty in the army. We understand some of the sacrifices that have to be made when serving overseas.

We are proud of the red, white and blue that runs through our veins, and we are aware of all that it takes to keep our country free. It is people like you that have given of yourself at the peril of your own life, and for the protection of others, that has made our country the great nation that it is. Our nation is a nation like no other. Our forefathers fought knowing that God was on their side, and it was He who inspired the constitution that we hold so dear.

These are difficult times, home and abroad. But we still belong to the greatest country on earth! Thank you for being one of the brave from the Land of the Free. We pray for your safety and if you are injured, we pray for a good and speedy recovery so that you may be able to return to your loved ones that you have left behind.

We are from a very small town in southern Idaho and there is a great deal of support in this area for those serving in the military at this time. You are not alone! Many, many thoughts and prayers go with you every day. We feel truly blessed to have people such as yourself who are willing to serve.

Thank you and may God bless you.

The Archibald Family.
Oakley, Idaho

Dear Service Member,

Life is good in Idaho—weather cold but sunny and bright. We see some good changes here—cheese factory going good in Burley, an ethanol plant to come here soon.

We are grateful to live in this great state with beautiful snowcapped mountains and the magnificent Snake River. The harvest was great last fall but 2007 should be even greater. How grateful we are to you to support our freedoms here and the privilege we have living in the "land of the free and the home of the brave."You are truly the brave ones. Thanks. We're proud of you. Our prayers go with you daily for your safety and strength to go on in the great cause of freedom throughout the world.

It would be wonderful if we were all united but I know that we support you and all the United States stands for. If politics and military would get together you'd be home soon.

God bless you,
Rollo and Gladys H.

P.S. We just returned from New Orleans, Louisiana. It sometimes looks like a war zone there with all the destruction from Hurricane Katrina, but it is also wonderful to see the young people come in and help clean out the homes and rebuild where they can. People in America are generally willing to help each other in time of need.

We pray the war could stop soon and then the rebuilding could come in and change the land into a beautiful homeland for the people in the war-torn territory in Iraq.

Dear Serviceman and Woman,

Just want you to know how much you are appreciated for all your efforts on our behalf.

I wish we could meet you sometime and express, personally, our gratitude.

I do hope things are going as well as possible for you. And do know you are in my—our—thoughts and prayers.

Best of luck to you now and always.

God bless,
Mayna M.

Dear Soldier,

Thanks so much for all you are doing to keep our land safe from terrorists. You are sacrificing your time and spending time away from your families and we could never thank you enough. My husband served time in the Second World War as a medic, then again in Korea. Looking over the ranks, he didn't recognize many—so many were different from when he was in the service.

What is the weather like there? How many children do you have? What are their interests? What did you do as a civilian?

Thank you again for what you are doing and may God bless you and your buddies. We love you.

Sincerely,
John and Mary Lou M.

Dear Soldier,

We can't tell you enough how much you all touch our hearts in the service you have done for our country and yours.

God bless you and keep you in His care. You all are in our prayers.

God's blessings on you.

The W. family
Burley, Idaho

Dear Service Member,

I want to thank you for your service and sacrifice to defend and protect our country and theirs.

I've had several members of my family in the military. They and you are all heroes to me.

It is cold here, but warm in this fellowship hall.

I spend my days caring for my husband, who was in the navy (submarines) for 20 years, and also my dogs.

We watch the news and it's hard to imagine what you are going through.

Stay strong! I hope you know how much we appreciate you.

Take care of yourself. I continue to pray for you and your safe return.

God bless you,
Joanne C.

To Any Service Person

We are grateful for the job you men and women are doing serving our country so that we might continue to have the freedoms that we now enjoy. May God bless and be near you, as you serve the greatest country on earth. This is written by the wife of a World War II veteran.

Thank you for your service,
Fred and Joyce P
Declo, Idaho

To Any Service Member,

Just wanted you to know that we appreciate your sacrifice of risking your life to try and make the world a better place. (Not only you, but your family that has to get along without you.)

We pray for, and are looking forward to a world of love, peace and harmony, and, hopefully, very soon! In the meantime, we ask for protection and help for you and all others that are in the forefront of the effort to bring this about. It may not come immediately, but you will eventually be blessed for your efforts!!

God bless you!!

A couple in Idaho (age 77 and 76)

Hi there,

I need to take a minute to thank you from the bottom of my heart for your selfless service in my behalf.

That you would volunteer is awesome. That you have set your life on hold, I am grateful that you do so. When a few are less grateful, [that] is disheartening.

Thank you for your service and devotion and the love of our country.

Keith R.

Dear Serviceman or Woman,

Just a note to let you know how very much you are appreciated! It's because of awesome young people like you that we enjoy the lifestyle we have.

We (my husband and I) are at a benefit dinner for "Operation Angel." It's so nice to be able to contribute in some small way. We pray for your efforts in all that you are doing. Hope the very best for you always.

It would be nice to be able to meet you and thank you personally.

God bless you,

M. M.

Dear Kevin and All Service Men and Women,

I hope for a moment you could pause and reflect and feel the love we send to you. I hope all of you are allowed to come home soon.

Sincerely,

Cynthia M.

Dearest Service Man/Woman,

I so much appreciate your sacrifice for me and all of us here in the USA. My husband, Keith, and I pray for you each night we kneel in prayer. We also pray for your families. What a sacrifice.

We pray that peace and democracy will bless the lives of the people there.

Thanks for caring—for your integrity, service, and for loving the sweet people and children there.

I pray for your safe return. I hope you say your prayers, too.

Take care,
Bev Ramsey

Hello there!

Greetings from Idaho!

Just a note to thank you for your service. You are much braver than I could ever be. I hope you are not wounded, but if you are my tears are for you and ask that you will be blessed with health and strength.

I hope you are safe. So much we see on the news is so sad.

Thank you for serving and defending our country. It is a great country and we want you to come home and be safe.

Our love to you and those you love!

D.A.D. family
Burley, Idaho

To Any Military Personnel,

A note to let you know that your sacrifice is a wonderful blessing. We enjoy so much in this country. I pray that you have a safe tour of duty. Please let your fellow soldiers know that we say "hello" and thank you, thank you, thank you.

With God's blessing to you,
Marsha G.
Heyburn, Idaho

To Any Service Person,

I want you to know how much I appreciate your sacrifice of time and effort in my behalf and that of my family. I know what it takes to be where you are today. My son is a Chief Petty Officer. I have two nephews in the army and a grandson in the navy. So stand proud but keep your head down low. Know that you are loved and in my prayers. You are important to me and all Americans who believe in the importance and responsibility of freedom.

If ever you are in Burley or Albion, Idaho, please call. I would like to give you a hug of appreciation.

Hang in there, be strong—we care.

Thank you for your efforts and may God bless you and yours.

With great respect,
Sharon H. M.

[I'm] proud of all you men and women who have put [your] life on hold and in harm's way for me and my family.

Thanks over and over again. I'm so proud to be an American!

We're here at a dinner to raise funds to put more gift bags together to show you all our hearts and thoughts are with you.

May God be with you 24-7.

Love to all,
Darla Y.

Dear Jarhead, Dogface, Swabby, Cloud Duster
or whatever,

Myself, I'm Jarhead (1957-1963).

I'm sitting here waiting for dinner with a large group of other old people. We're here to listen to the success of the "2006 Project Rudolph." You are receiving this letter as a small part of the effort.

This dinner is also to raise funds for "2007 Project Rudolph," which will bring some pleasure to you and other service people.

Myself, I have great respect for you and any active military in harm's way. I wish you the best and God's love. All of you are frequently in our prayers.

Orlo Y.

Dear Soldier,

Just a note to let you know how much I appreciate your service to our country. Even though you aren't at home, you're in my thoughts and prayers.

My dad served in the army in World War II. His military service was a high point in his life and he was very proud of it. I still hold appreciation and respect for our service personnel that he taught me.

You have my prayers for your safety and that the military can accomplish their purpose. May you have the strength and inspiration to do what you must.

Linda from Idaho

Hi there, dear soldier,

Can you believe that the first month of the year has come and gone already? How are you doing? We appreciate everything you do for our freedoms. I know that I'm quoting a line from a song, but it is because of you we can sleep in peace at night.

I imagine your friends and family are very proud of you, but miss you terribly. Hopefully you will be able to go home soon.

It is beginning to warm up here. Hopefully it continues, because it has been so cold for so long. I don't know what the weather is like over there, but I hope it is comfortable for you and your troops.

We love you all. Stay safe and know you are always in our prayers.

Ardell M.

Dear Soldier,

I don't know who you are or where you are, but I do know that you are somewhere in this small world of ours working to preserve the freedoms of America. Not only America, but citizens of other countries who long to have the same freedoms we enjoy.

Without our service men and women from the army, navy, air force, marines, etc., we probably would not be a free nation at the present time. I just want to thank you for the part you have had in preserving my freedom. I'll keep you in my prayers.

I'm an 81-year-old grandmother and consider all service men and women my grandchildren.

Clara from Idaho

Dear Service Member,

Thank you so much for what you do for our great country! It is something I can't do, and I appreciate it so much! My father was in the military as well as my two brothers-in-law. We are so grateful for your service and sacrifice for me and my family.

God bless you and yours.

Thanks,

David K. and family

To Any Service Member,

Thanks a million.

From Michael M.

Dear Service Member,

We would like to thank you for your service and sacrifice for our country. Please know that our soldiers who are serving and their families left behind are in our thoughts and prayers daily. Your efforts are not forgotten. We truly appreciate what you are doing.

Thank you for being an example to our youth. Whether people believe in this war or not, they see that soldiers are willing to fight to help make lives better for others who cannot help themselves.

May God bless you that you will have the strength to carry out your duties and return home. May He bless your family that they will be comforted in your absence and that they will remain strong and that their needs will be met.

We wish you a safe and happy return!

With heartfelt thanks,
The Radicic Family
West Point, New York

Dear Service Member,

Thank you so much for serving our country during these difficult times. I appreciate all you do to fight terrorism and keep America and the rest of the world safe. Your sacrifices are many and sometimes they may seem thankless; however, please know that millions of Americans, like myself, are grateful for you and your service to our country. Love,

Linda Renz

Dear Service Man or Woman,

I want to thank you for your sacrifice. I am grateful for the freedom that you help provide through your service. I pray that Heavenly Father will protect you and keep you out of harm, and that you can return to your family soon. Please know there are many here at home praying for your safety and quick return. Your willingness to serve our country will be a blessing to all Americans and the Iraqi people.

Thank you for all you are doing to bring democracy and freedom to oppressed people there.

Sincerely,
Jae Mason

Dear Serviceman,

Greetings from Idaho! As this Christmas season approaches and our family stops to consider our great blessings, we must be grateful for our selfless service men and women. What great respect we have for you and the duties you perform for others. Truly, there is no greater sacrifice than he who gives of his time, talents and life for another. We appreciate you, we honor you, we pray for you and your family. May your time and energies be rewarded. May your experiences be fulfilling and safe.

Again, we thank you for your willingness to serve this great country of ours. And from a little town in southern Idaho, we offer you our most grateful thanks. As we have taken an evening, as a family, to write to you it has been a good experience to share with our four children about the courageous servicemen overseas.

I have included one of my favorite quotations.

"There are two ways of exerting one's strength. One is pushing down and the other is pulling up."

– Booker T. Washington

Sincerely,
Debbie Critchfield

My name is Tara. I live with my husband, Andrew; my one-year-old miniature Schnauzer, Jocque; and we are awaiting the birth of our first child in January. I just want you to know, even thought I don't know who you are or where you're from, I appreciate you and what you do for me, my family and my country. You are a lot braver than I am and I look up to you for what you do. I hope this letter brings you comfort and joy while you are away from your family. You are in our prayers. Continue to stay safe and best wishes while you are in the service of your country. We all truly appreciate the things you do for all of us.

Tara C.

To a Service Man or Woman,

Hope you're in a place where you can have a good Christmas and able to help others do the same.

I have a soft place in my heart for anyone that is defending this great country we have to live in and the freedoms we have. Yes, I am a veteran from World

War II and I remember how proud I was to fight for our freedom we and others are able to enjoy. May your Xmas be filled with joy and happiness and your return home soon.

I ask the Lord's blessings to be with you at all times and remember we are all very proud of you and what you're fighting for. May Old Glory fly forever over this great country we live in!! May God bless!!!

Always a friend,
Dallan Elquist

To Whoever Receives This Letter,

Your devotion and service on all our behalves is acknowledged and very much appreciated. You may not hear this as much as you should, but that doesn't diminish the importance of what you do. I hope your family and friends are also proud of you. My prayers are with you this day and I hope you travel in safety.

Sincerely,
Kerry Anderson

I just wanted to thank you for the service you are providing for our country. It is very much appreciated. It must be so hard to be away from your family during this time, but we are so very grateful for what you are doing. I may not have the opportunity to meet you in this life, but know that we are thinking about you and you are in our prayers. Thanks again for everything you are doing and I hope you are well and happy.

Thank you for everything that you have done to keep this country safe. I don't think that I could leave my family and go to a foreign country and fight for my country. I appreciate everything that you and many others have done!

Sincerely,
Robert Mason

Dear Soldier,

My name is Amanda. In my spare time I like to cheer. My favorite colors are pink and orange. I hate school! Busses are dumb. I don't like my parents and they don't like me. My mom is 29 and my dad is 27. I have three cats. They are stupid, but I love them. Do you have a husband or a wife? Do you have kids? Is a soldier supposed to be smart? 'Cause if they are, I can't join the army. My gramma is in the army, but she died last year. I have a pledge for her. Wanna hear it? Okay.

"I pledge allegiance to my gramma who lives in the grave with my grampa who was in the army."

I want to be in the army.

Thank you for your time.

Sincerely,
Amanda

About the Compiler

Tawny Archibald Campbell began her writing career at the age of 18 when she was hired to work for a small Idaho newspaper right out of high school. She has continued her newspaper career by working as a writer and photographer off and on for the last 10 years for both civilian and military newspapers.

In 2001 her husband and best friend, Joe, joined the Army and together they began the adventure of their lives. Two years later a daughter, Ceilidha, was born and the fun continued. The family has moved 10 times in the past seven years and is currently stationed in Germany where Tawny has begun three different charities, all supporting military service men and women.

This book is a way of sharing her love of the military with the world, and proceeds from the book will go towards continuing Operation Angel and Project Portrait.

For more information go to www.operationangel.homestead.com or www.projectportrait.homestead.com. You can e-mail Tawny at taznjo@hotmail.com.